"Atheism Remix offers a masterful analysis of and timely response to the New Atheism. Thoughtful and insightful, this readable work illuminates for scholars, pastors, and students alike the key issues that must be addressed in order to engage the thinking of Dawkins, Harris, Hitchens, and others. I applaud Albert Mohler for his clarity and conviction in helping us understand that biblical theism is the only true alternative to the New Atheism. I gladly recommend this book!"

—DAVID S. DOCKERY, President, Union University

"The great strength of these lectures-turned-book is the sweep of their coverage. Instead of becoming just one more voice in the rising debate between Christians and the New Atheists, Dr. Mohler has chosen to provide us with masterful coverage of the dominant writers on both sides. I happily attest how accurate and penetrating are Mohler's surveys and assessments. I know of no other introduction to this crucial debate that is as comprehensive and clear in such brief compass. Mohler tells us what's going on, shows us how much depends on the outcome of this titanic cultural shift, and provides guidance to the resources Christians need to challenge the New Atheism root and branch."

—D. A. CARSON, Research Professor of
New Testament, Trinity Evangelical Divinity School

"The New Atheism needs a clear-headed, straightforward analysis. *Atheism Remix* does this, and it does it well. Al Mohler is clear and concise in his critique, and the readability of this book makes it accessible to a wide audience. This is a fine introduction and overview of the self-proclaimed 'Four Horsemen' of atheism. They are examined, and their arguments are exposed as vacuous."

—DANIEL AKIN, President, Southeastern Baptist
Theological Seminary

atheism R E M I X

Crossway books with contributions by R. Albert Mohler Jr.:

By Faith Alone: Answering the Challenges to the Doctrine of Justification

Whatever Happened to Truth?

The Glory of Christ

The Compromised Church: The Present Evangelical Crisis

Who Will Be Saved? Defending the Biblical Understanding of God, Salvation, and Evangelism

atheism REMIX
A Christian Confronts the New Atheists

R. Albert Mohler Jr.

CROSSWAY BOOKS

WHEATON, ILLINOIS

PDF ISBN: 978-1-4335-0498-3

Mobipocket ISBN: 978-1-4335-0499-0

Library of Congress Cataloging-in-Publication Data
Mohler, R. Albert, 1959–
   Atheism remix : a Christian confronts the new atheists /
R. Albert Mohler.
      p. cm.
   ISBN 978-1-4335-0497-6 (hc)
   1. Christianity and atheism. I. Title.
BR128.A8M64   2008
261.2'1—dc22   2008014228

LB		17	16	15	14	13	12	11	10	09	08
14	13	12	11	10	9	8	7	6	5	4	3	2	1

To
my parents,

DICK and JANET MOHLER,

Who grounded me in the faith,
Sustained me with love, and
Encouraged my questions.

Contents

Introduction

A theism is not a new concept. Even the Bible speaks of the one who tells himself in his heart, "There is no God."[1] Atheism became an organized and publicly recognized worldview in the wake of the Enlightenment and has maintained a foothold in Western culture ever since. Disbelief in God became part of the cultural landscape in the 1960s when *Time* magazine published a cover story—"Is God Dead?"— that seemed to herald the arrival of a new secular age.[2]

Nevertheless, atheists have represented only a small (if vocal) minority of Americans. Surveys estimate that atheists represent less than 2 percent of the population, even as the larger group of "unaffiliated" includes over 15 percent. Atheists have published books, held seminars, presented their views in the media, and honed their points in public debates. As a worldview, atheism is overrepresented among the intellectual elites, and atheists have largely, though not exclusively, talked to their own.

Until now. Get on an airplane, settle in for a flight,

---

[1] Psalm 14:1.
[2] *Time*, April 8, 1966.

and observe what other passengers are reading. You are likely to see books representing a new wave of atheism as you look around the cabin. The so-called New Atheists have written bestsellers that have reached far beyond the traditional audience for such books. Books by Richard Dawkins and Christopher Hitchens have spent weeks and months on the best-seller list published by the *New York Times*. Clearly, something is happening.

* * *

The New Atheism is not just a reassertion of atheism. It is a movement that represents a far greater public challenge to Christianity than that posed by the atheistic movements of previous times. Furthermore, the New Atheism is not just another example of marketing an idea in the postmodern age. The New Atheists are, in their own way, evangelistic in intent and ambitious in hope. They see atheism as the only plausible worldview for our times, and they see belief in God as downright dangerous—an artifact of the past that we can no longer afford to tolerate, much less encourage.

They see science as on their side and argue that scientific knowledge is our only true knowledge. They argue that belief in God is organized ignorance, that theistic beliefs lead to violence, and that atheism is liberation. They are shocked and appalled that Americans refuse to follow the predictions of the secularization theorists, who had assured the elites that belief in God would be dissolved by the acids of modernity. They have added new (and very important) arguments to the atheistic arsenal. They write from positions of privilege, and they know how to package their ideas. They know that the most important audience is the young, and they are in a position to reach young people with their arguments.

The New Atheists represent a major challenge to the Christian church and to Christian theology. *Atheism Remix* is based upon the W. H. Griffith Thomas Lectures delivered in 2008 at Dallas Theological Seminary. Dr. Griffith Thomas was one of the key founders of Dallas Theological Seminary and a staunch defender of the Christian faith. If alive today, he would undoubtedly see the New Atheism as a theological challenge that calls for our active engagement and most careful thought. He would be right.

I express appreciation to President Mark Bailey and the faculty of Dallas Theological Seminary for the invitation to deliver the 2008 W. H. Griffith Thomas Lectures and to the students for their respectful and interested listening. They, along with the students I see every day at The Southern Baptist Theological Seminary, represent the generation that cannot avoid engagement with the New Atheism. It is not going to go away any time soon.

I also want to express appreciation to Greg Gilbert, director of research in my office, who has been of such great assistance in my lectures and writings, and to the many friends and colleagues who have sharpened my thinking on this new challenge.

As always, I am thankful for my wife, Mary, without whose constant support and care none of these things would ever see the light of day, and to our children, Katie and Christopher, who love me and make me laugh.

The New Atheism and
the Endgame of Secularism

everal years ago, I attended a lecture in which I seized upon a thought that has never left me. The lecturer was Doctor Heiko Obermann, the great and now late historian of the late Medieval and early Reformation eras. In the midst of his lecture, he looked out at the audience, paused, reflected, and then said, and I paraphrase, "I can see that you do not understand what I am saying to you. What I am saying to you is that you do not live life as Martin Luther lived life. You do not wake up in the morning as he did, nor do you go to bed at night as he did. You need to understand something about changed conditions of belief. Do you not understand that in the time of Martin Luther, almost every single human being in European civilization woke up afraid that he would die before nightfall? Eternal destiny was a daily, hourly, minute-by-minute thought. Every night, as the late Medieval or early Reformation human being closed his eyes, he feared that he would wake up either in heaven or in hell. You do not live with that fear. And that means that your understanding of these things is very different from Martin Luther's. That's why he threw ink pots at the Devil, and you close your notebook and sleep well at night."

This whole idea of "changed conditions of belief" takes on new importance when we consider the movement that we now call the New Atheism. Something has happened in our culture, and it is now impossible to miss. Something has changed, and that change can be easily measured by the sales of books. The sales figures of books written by the New Atheists—the most notable being Richard Dawkins, Daniel Dennett, Sam Harris, and Christopher Hitchens—are simply astounding. Their books are selling by the millions, and three of these authors have produced books that remained on the *New York Times'* best-seller list for a matter of months, not weeks. In the history of books about atheism nothing like this has ever happened. Atheism has long had a niche audience, but it has now become a mass phenomenon in terms of publishing and media attention.

Not too long ago, I had a conversation with a network news anchor in which he made the off-hand comment, "If I were you, I would give these fellows a great deal of attention." When a network news anchor is advising theologians to give attention to a cultural movement, it is indeed probably time to start paying attention. The prominence of the New Atheists in the media, multiplied by their influence among the academic and intellectual elites, means that the New Atheism presents a significant challenge to Christian theology—a challenge that demands our closest attention.

*   *   *

One of the key questions to ask about the New Atheism is, "What makes the New Atheism *new*?" Before launching too far into our interaction with this new challenge, we should recognize something from the very outset: atheism is not new. David said in the psalms, "The fool says in his heart, there is no God," (Ps. 14:1). Even that statement, however, assumes something different from what faces us today. In the ancient world and throughout most of human history, the question was never whether or not there *is* a God, but which god is God? Thus, in the Old Testament, one of God's most insistent purposes is to make clear that he is the *only* God, and that he will tolerate no other. That is a very different question from what is being asked today.

The word *atheism* did not appear in the English language until the sixteenth century. The *Oxford English Dictionary* documents the first use of the word to 1568, when it was coined (or borrowed from another language) by Miles Coverdale. In a fairly short time, the word made its way into more common usage. Even then,

it was used to describe a phenomenon that was thought
to be very new—the denial of belief in God. The out-
ward, straightforward, public rejection of belief in theism was so new at that time that it required a new word.
It's interesting to note that this happened in the wake
of what is now known as the Elizabethan Settlement.
Elizabeth I of Great Britain decided to settle the strife
of the Reformation struggles by declaring a sort of religious toleration. "I do not intend to make windows into
men's souls," she famously said. As a result, there was
loosed within English society a degree of religious plu-
ralism that had not existed before, including some on
the periphery of society—mostly limited to the intellectual elite and some cultural cranks—who denied belief
in any God. These people were considered dangerous
and worthy of ostracism. In fact, they were considered
worthy of a new word: *atheists*. Yet even after the emergence of the word in the English language there were
very few people who actually denied belief in God.

Unsurprisingly, it is only after the Enlightenment
that atheism became a real intellectual force. The
Enlightenment produced a massive shift in the conditions of belief. In the great turn to the subject, in the
division between the phenomenal and the noumenal,
as Kant famously construed it, even in the rise of
historical analysis and modern science, there was a
great epistemological shift in Western consciousness,
and the result was a new opportunity for the denial of

belief in the supernatural in general and the denial of a personal supernatural God specifically. Doubt came to be considered as an intellectual tool, and there arose a culture of doubt and skepticism. In the period from the sixteenth to the eighteenth century, the conditions of belief changed dramatically.

One way to understand what happened is to consider what kind of god was left in the wake of Enlightenment thought. For example, if you consider carefully the philosophy of Immanuel Kant, it is clear that he believed in God. But it is not clear at all that he believed in a supernatural, personal God—and certainly not in a God who intervenes in human history. What was left in the wake of the Enlightenment was no longer a fairly monolithic affirmation of theism, but rather a plethora of movements that also included skeptics and freethinkers, as well as Deists and pantheists.

In the late nineteenth century we finally arrive at the four horsemen of the modern apocalypse—Friedrich Nietzsche, Karl Marx, Charles Darwin, and Sigmund Freud. To mention those four names together is to represent a massive cultural, intellectual, and epistemological shift. Each of these men contributed to human thought in a way that changed the conditions of belief, the intellectual foundations of all thought.

Take Sigmund Freud for example. The unconscious, Freud said, explains more than does the conscious. Indeed, it is the precondition of the conscious. Given that, it is easy to see why Freud would believe that religion is merely an illusion that would eventually pass away. Long before Freud came the publication in 1859 of Charles Darwin's book *The Descent of Man*.[1] From 1859 until the death of Freud at the beginning of the Second World War, an entire change of thinking had taken place, at least among the intellectual classes. Nietzsche, of course, the most abrupt and abrasive of these thinkers, actually celebrated the death of God. In his book *The Gay Science,* Nietzsche declared flatly that "God is dead," which was his way of saying that belief in the Christian God had become unbelievable.[2] In his work *The Anti-Christ*, he went on to write that the worst enemy of human enlightenment and progress is the Christian. He refers to Christianity and to Christians in particular as the "domestic animal, the herd animal, the sick animal—the Christian."[3] He said:

> Christianity has taken the side of everything weak, base, failed; it has made an ideal out of whatever *contradicts* the preservation instincts of a strong life; it has corrupted the reason of even the most spiritual natures by teaching people to see the highest spiritual values as sinful, as deceptive, as *tempta-*

[1]Charles Darwin, *The Descent of Man: Selection in Relation to Sex* (Penguin, 2004).
[2]Friedrich Wilhelm Nietzsche, *The Gay Science: With a Prelude in German Rhymes and an Appendix of Songs*. Cambridge Texts in the History of Philosophy (Cambridge: Cambridge University Press, 2001).
[3]Friedrich Wilhelm Nietzsche, *The Anti-Christ, Ecce Homo, Twilight of the Idols and Other Writings*, ed. Aaron Ridley and Judith Norman (Cambridge: Cambridge University Press, 2005), 4–5.

tions. The most pitiful example—the corruption of Pascal, who believed that his reason was corrupted by original sin when the only thing corrupting it was Christianity itself![4]

So Nietzsche declared war on theology:

I wage war on this theologian instinct: I have found traces of it everywhere. Anyone with theologian blood in his veins will approach things with a warped and deceitful attitude. This gives rise to a pathos that calls itself *faith*: turning a blind eye to yourself once and for all, so you do not have to stomach the sight of incurable mendacity.[5]

And:

The Christian idea of God—God as a god of the sick, God as spider, God as spirit—is one of the most corrupt conceptions of God the world has ever seen; this may even represent a new low in the declining development of the types of god. God having degenerated into a *contradiction of life* instead of its transfiguration and eternal *yes*. God as declared aversion to life, to nature, to the will to life. God as the formula for every slander against "the here and now," for every lie about the "beyond." God as the deification of nothingness, the canonization of the will to nothingness![6]

[4]Ibid., 5.
[5]Ibid., 8.
[6]Ibid., 15–16.

In one famous essay he ends with these words: "And all the while, this pathetic God of Christian monotono-theism instead, acting as if it had any right to exist, like an *ultimatum* and *maximum* of god-creating energy, of the human *creator sprititus*! this hybrid creature of ruin, made from nullity, concept, and contradiction, who sanctions all the instincts of decadence, all the coward-ices and exhaustions of the soul!"[7] Nietzsche declares the necessity of God's death in order for humans to find liberation in this new intellectual age. He also suggested that Christianity itself was a vile and pathetic faith that produced vile and pathetic creatures. Any creature, he said, who would need belief in God—any creature who would need prayer, any creature who would exercise faith—is a creature whose will is so corrupted by the virus of Christianity that it cannot contribute to society and the building of a strong people.[8]

It is fairly clear, in retrospect, where Nietzsche's philosophy led. It led to nihilism and eventually to the Third Reich. Even so, Nietzsche is one of the most cel-ebrated figures in intellectual life today, a fact borne out by the sheer number of dissertations being written these days on Nietzsche and his heirs such as Michel Foucault. Nietzsche's radicalism makes him one of the most fascinating figures in modern thought. He believed himself to be declaring what should be obvious

---

[7]Ibid., 16.
[8]Ibid.

to all, and he was confident that others *did* see what he saw but were too timid or intellectually fearful to declare themselves.

If anything, Nietzsche's atheism serves to remind us all that atheism has consequences. As we shall see, one of the features of the New Atheism that seems most perplexing is its cultural cheerfulness. The New Atheists seem genuinely to believe that God is dead, but that humanity can now move cheerily along into a brave secular future. Nietzsche knew that atheism would be very costly—and very dangerous.

*   *   *

One of the fascinating themes to note in all this is what historians now call the "Victorian Loss of Faith." This is the context in which the word *atheism* becomes far more widespread, indicating a change in the mentality of very many people who lived in Victorian England. We tend to look back to Victorian England and note the overt religiosity of the era—the great churches, the great preachers like Charles Spurgeon, and the publicity given to Anglican luminaries. But what you might miss if you are not careful is that the Victorian era also saw a significant slide from Christian belief, famously encapsulated in the British motto, "My mind is no longer a Christian even though my body is."

In other words, a person can continue to *live* as

a Christian without believing anymore in the basic
tenets of the faith, even in the existence of God himself.
One symbolic figure of that era is the Reverend Leslie
Stephen, who was the father of the writer Virginia
Woolf. Stephen was an orthodox Anglican pastor who
lost his faith, resigned his orders, left the church, and
thus became a symbol of the Victorian loss of faith within
British intellectual thought.[9] This loss of faith was per-
haps best expressed in poetry, for example in Thomas
Hardy's poem "God's Funeral." Hardy wrote:

> *And, tricked by our own early dream*
> *And need of solace, we grew self-deceived,*
> *Our making soon our maker did we deem,*
> *And what we had imagined we believed,*
> *'Till, in Time's stayless stealthy swing,*
> *Uncompromising rude reality*
> *Mangled the Monarch of our fashioning,*
> *Who quavered, sank; and now has ceased to be.*
> *'So, toward our myth's oblivion,*
> *Darkling, and languid-lipped, we creep and grope*
> *Sadlier than those who wept in Babylon,*
> *Whose Zion was a still abiding hope.*
> *'How sweet it was in years far hied*
> *To start the wheels of day with trustful prayer,*
> *To lie down liegely at the eventide*
> *And feel a blest assurance he was there!*
> *'And who or what shall fill his place?*
> *Whither will wanderers turn distracted eyes*

[9] A. N. Wilson, *God's Funeral* (New York: Norton, 1999), 8–11.

For some fixed star to stimulate their pace
Towards the goal of their enterprise?'

And then later:

I could not prop their faith: and yet
Many I had known: with all I sympathized;
And though struck speechless, I did not forget
That what was mourned for, I, too, once had prized.

One of the most notable hallmarks of this Victorian loss of faith is a sense of mourning. That is extremely important, because it is conspicuously lacking in the New Atheism. Among the New Atheists, there is no sense of mourning something that was lost, no sense that something precious is now gone. Instead, there is actually a sense of celebration that theism is finally left behind.

The sense of mourning was also captured in another, equally famous, poem—Matthew Arnold's *Dover Beach*. He writes:

The Sea of Faith
Was once, too, at the full, and round earth's shore
Lay like the folds of a bright girdle furled.
But now I only hear
Its melancholy, long, withdrawing roar,
Retreating, to the breath
Of the night wind, down the vast edges drear

And naked shingles of the world.
Ah, love, let us be true
To one another! for the world, which seems
To lie before us like a land of dreams,
So various, so beautiful, so new,
Hath really neither joy, nor love, nor light,
Nor certitude, nor peace, nor help for pain;
And we are here as on a darkling plain
Swept with confused alarms of struggle and flight,
Where ignorant armies clash by night.

The sense of absence here is palpable. The One who once had been here, who had defined all of reality, was now gone, no longer accessible and no longer existent. And that absence of God began to define everything the Victorian intellectual knew.

In the twentieth century, the Victorian loss of faith was codified intellectually, first in the philosophy of logical positivism and secondly in protest atheism. It's interesting to note that the Holocaust became—along with the other unspeakable tragedies of the twentieth century—the great cause of much protest atheism. Evil became a catalyst for a form of atheism that argues that if there is a God, he cannot be a God like this. If this is God, then there is no God. In his play *J.B.*, Archibald MacLeish has his character, speaking in the form of Job, say, "If God is God He is not good, If God is good He is not God."[10] For many, the events of the twentieth

---

[10]Archibald MacLeish, *J.B.: A Play in Verse* (Boston: Houghton Mifflin, 1958), 11.

century—in particular the Holocaust and those two murderous World Wars—seemed to prove that point beyond doubt.

*   *   *

There was also in the early twentieth century the rise of the explicitly atheistic state. The Russian Revolution in 1917, and successive revolutions as well, produced the first atheistic states. Tsar Nicholas II had not only been Tsar of all the Russias, but also the titular head of the Russian Orthodox Church. Now, however, the state was explicitly atheistic and dedicated to Marx's assumption that religion is "the opiate of the masses."[11] And as the cultural elites saw it, that opiate must be taken from the people and replaced with the vision of the new Communist man.

After World War II, the West accelerated toward modernity, particularly in terms of technology and science. Great social changes affected the way most people in the West lived. People became more mobile than ever before, which led to unprecedented levels of social dislocation and, in turn, to the demise of the extended family. No longer was it natural for successive generations of the extended family to live together under one roof. Personal autonomy began to be prized, the therapeutic

---

[11]Karl Marx, *Critique of Hegel's Philosophy of Right,* trans. Annette Jolin and Joseph O'Malley (Cambridge: Cambridge University Press, 1970).

culture started to take hold, and the elites of culture became increasingly secularized. By the time we reach hyper-modernity, after the atom was split and Sputnik was launched, after vaccines were invented and man had stood on the moon, there was a sense that human beings, much like Nietzsche's prototypical human, had finally come of age. People began to believe that God is simply no longer necessary.

Then arises the postmodern era, in which the very foundations of theism are denied, along with all other foundationalist thinking. God is made merely one thought among other thoughts, one principle among other principles, one socially constructed reality among others. And in the midst of this arise the New Atheists.

*   *   *

I believe that what we see in the rise of the New Atheism is something of the endgame of secularism. In order to understand this, we must look at the origins of what is known as secularization theory.

The idea of secularization emerged from early socio-logical analysis. It was thought that as modernity worked its way through civilization, as human beings learned to harness the energies of nature, dam rivers, and eventually split the atom, there would be less and less need for God as the causal, explanatory factor in the intellectual framework of civilization. As the secularization theorists saw the future, life would become increasingly rationalized. More and more of life would be experienced in a secular space, and belief in God, along with participation in organized religion, would dissipate. Inevitably then, God would recede from human consciousness.

Max Weber spoke of this process as "disenchantment."[12] Eventually modernity would lead to society's disenchantment with the enchanted world, by which he meant a world in which God is necessary and meaningful, and its entrance into a disenchanted (or secular) world. Emile Durkheim predicted the same, as did Auguste Comte. Modernity was understood as humanity come of age, and religious faith and belief in God were seen as recidivist, backward, and limiting beliefs that would inevitably recede.

Lying behind the secularization theory were two great assumptions: first, the theory assumes that theism is basically an inherited belief that is necessary to provide meaning, coherence, and comfort. In other words, secularization theory has an essentially functional understanding of religion. So, as religion's function is no longer needed, as people find other sources of comfort and meaning in life, belief in God will recede.

Second, secularization theory assumes that the

---

[12]Max Weber, *The Protestant Ethic and the Spirit of Capitalism*, ed. Stephen Kalberg (New York: Oxford University Press, 2001).

forms of religious belief were supported by the acknowl-
edgment of its social functions. In other words, the
adherents of secularization theory believed that religious forms would remain for some time even after true
belief was gone—at least so long as people found them
aesthetically attractive—but that eventually they also
would disappear. They believed history was driving
toward the utter removal of belief in God, and that education, technology, affluence, and the inevitable breaks
with tradition that came with modernity would lead to
a massive, civilization-wide loss of belief.

It would work this way: first it would become *plausible* or thinkable not to believe in God, and then eventually it would become *inevitable* that one would not
believe in God at all. Secularization theorists believed
education would play a big role in this, effecting in
society an intellectual coming of age. In sum, belief in
God was a part of prehistory, a part of what Nietzsche
would call "the intellectual infancy of humanity." But
as humanity has now come of age, belief in God is no
longer necessary. Freud put it this way: "The more the
fruits of knowledge become accessible to men, the more
widespread is the decline of religious belief."[13]

Ultimately then, modernity would produce a fully
secularized world. On a global scale it would begin in
the West, where technology, scientific advance, and
democratic theory had most quickly taken shape. But

---

[13]Sigmund Freud, *Future of an Illusion* (New York: Norton, 1989).

eventually these ideas would spread around the world, and secularization would be a global phenomenon. The theory certainly appeared to be credible, and it soon became the accepted wisdom. Indeed, it was considered to be inexorable: there would be a worldwide, global, secular culture, led by new institutions such as the United Nations and marked by the rejection of both the social functions and the symbolic nature of theistic belief.

*   *   *

John Sommerville, another major British figure in secularization theory, suggested that secularization would follow this pattern: first would come the secularization of space. In the year 1500 in Great Britain, about half of all the land in the kingdom was owned by the church, and a good portion of the rest was owned by the Crown. That began to change with Henry VIII, who confiscated the monasteries and began the process of secularizing the property. The idea that land would not be owned by either the Church or the Crown was a massive change in British society. Second, Sommerville predicted the secularization of time and play, and third, the secularization of language. Fourth was the secularization of technology and work. No longer would people consider their vocation as being done to the glory of God. Rather, the dominant paradigm would be that of making a contribution to society and ultimately a profit. Then would follow the secularization of art, the secularization of power, the secularization of personhood and association, and finally the secularization of scholarship and science until humanity's passage from infancy and adolescence into adulthood was complete.

Sommerville went on to speak of six aspects of secularization. First, secularization would take place at the macro-social-institutional level. This is known as *differentiation*. This process has clearly become a reality. Indeed, the fragmentation of knowledge and the specialization of expertise are now just taken for granted. Whereas the church once defined reality across an entire range of intellectual fields, it does so no longer—even for most Christians. We live in a time in which it is plausible to us that people would not ask the pastor about vocational issues, intellectual issues, legal issues, and all the rest. The church used to be at the center of all these questions, but differentiation now means that you go to a lawyer for legal advice and to a psychotherapist for counseling. People now go to any number of experts who are completely freed from the church and theistic belief. That is a massive shift brought about by secularization.

Second, secularization affects individual institutions. Think of all the universities and hospitals once established explicitly as Christian, which are now fully secularized. The most significant dimension of this institutional secularization has to do with the secularization of the academy. The secularization of colleges and universities has shaped the minds and worldviews of millions.[14] Third, activities such as education and welfare, which used to be done by the church and in the name of the church, have now largely been taken over by the bureaucratic state. Fourth, Sommerville argued, mentalities and worldviews would be secularized. At the level of worldview, basic presuppositional ideas would be secularized and, almost imperceptibly, the mind would be secularized. Fifth, entire peoples would be secularized in terms of belief and identity. They would, like Europe today, desperately strive to separate themselves from their Christian heritage. Finally, Sommerville even talks about the secularization of religion, the attempt to accommodate theology to a secularized world.[15]

There were of course some scholars who did not go along. By 1986, Jeffrey Hadden would say that secularization was more a doctrine than a theory: it too had to be taken on faith.[16] But even more problematic for the theory is the fact that it simply isn't happening—at least not as the secularization theorists said it

---

[14]See George M. Marsden, *The Soul of the American University: From Protestant Establishment to Established Non-Belief* (New York: Oxford University Press, 1994) and James Tunstead Burtchaell, *The Dying of the Light: The Disengagement of Colleges and Universities from Their Christian Churches* (Grand Rapids, MI: Eerdmans, 1998).

[15]C. John Sommerville, *The Secularization of Early Modern England: From Religious Culture to Religious Faith* (New York: Oxford University Press, 1992).

[16]Jeffrey Hadden, 1986 Presidential Address to the Southern Sociological Society.

would happen. Take the United States of America, for example, the most hyper-modern state in the world as measured by sociological analysis. Ninety-five percent of Americans claim to believe in God. Now obviously the god in whom these people believe is not necessarily the God of biblical theism. But even so, Americans by and large are *not* secularists. Furthermore, instead of the spread of a global phenomenon of secularization, there appears to be a reassertion of religious belief around the world. So what happened?

What happened is that the theory of secularization soon became known as the "myth" of secularization. Peter Berger, who was one of the initial framers of the entire idea of secularization theory, has been very helpful in coming back to acknowledge that the theory must be recalibrated.[17] At the same time, however, we must recognize that there is still something to the theory— even in its classical form. Secularization theory may have been falsified in terms of its major claims, but there are still two senses in which it was *exactly* right.

The first sense in which secularization theory was right is geographic. Western Europe followed the theory perfectly. Rates of church-going in Germany, Sweden, the Netherlands, Spain, and France hover right around 1 to 5 percent of the population. In many surveys, fewer than 10 percent of those populations claim to believe in God. The second exception to secularization theory's

---

[17]See Peter C. Berger, "Secularization Falsified," *First Things*, February 2008, 23f.

failure is among the world's cultural and intellectual elites. Here Peter Berger has put it wonderfully. In the course of studying the relative levels of religious belief in the world's countries, sociologists determined that the least religious nation in the world was Sweden, while the most religious was India. Berger, speaking of the United States, said that what we have in America is a nation of Indians ruled over by an elite of Swedes. As Berger has explained, the secularized global intelligentsia is in all nations a minority of the population, "but a very influential one."[18]

The significance of these two exceptions is that Western Europe and the world's cultural elites play an inordinate role in influencing the larger culture. Thus the secularization of Europe and of America's elites has created a cultural opening for the emergence of what we are calling the New Atheism. How exactly has this opening occurred?

* * *

Perhaps the most insightful philosopher to have considered this is Charles Taylor. His massive work *A Secular Age* is a bold but also rather humble and honest work.[19] Taylor has given attention over the decades to the secularization of society and to what it means to live

---

[18]Ibid., 24.
[19]Charles Taylor, *A Secular Age* (Cambridge, MA: Belknap Press, 2007).

in a secular age, and he makes an argument that is very difficult to refute. Taylor's argument is that Western history has experienced three different intellectual stages, three different sets of conditions of belief.

First, there once was a time in which it was impossible *not* to believe. If you move back before the Enlightenment, into the Medieval period and beyond, it was virtually impossible to find persons who did not believe in God, or who at least did not assume that belief in God was absolutely necessary in order to make sense of the world. Believing in God was crucial to understanding why the sun was there in the morning and the moon and the stars at night. God was an integral, inseparable part of society's *Weltanschauung*, its worldview. It was impossible not to believe because there was no other explanation. There was no other theory, no other rival worldview that could explain all that human beings experienced.

The second phase Taylor describes is when it becomes *possible* not to believe. The Enlightenment becomes the great opening for this, for even though it remained, for most people, still impossible not to believe, the great epistemological turn to the subject meant that the possibility of nonbelief suddenly emerged. The individual himself became the center of meaning, and thus God was no longer understood to be the sovereign subject, but rather the object of study. And like any other theory, one could take him or leave him.

Taylor suggests that we have now entered a third stage of intellectual development. Having moved from a time in which it was impossible not to believe, through a time in which it became possible not to believe, we have now arrived at a situation in which, for the elites especially, it has become impossible *to believe*. If you compare the first stage and the third stage, an absolute reversal has taken place. In the first stage there was no rival explanation for any reality—for life, for the past, for the present, or for the future—other than Christianity. But now it is the absolute opposite. Now there are not only alternatives to the biblical worldview available, but these alternatives are declared to be superior. Indeed if nonbelief was an oddity in the first stage—so much that it was considered eccentric and even dangerous—in this third stage it is *theism* that is considered eccentric and dangerous. Theism is not just something we have moved beyond, not just something we ought to put behind us as belonging to an infantile or adolescent period of human development. It is actually dangerous, because people who believe in God are dangerous people who do dangerous things. They are a deadly toxin within the culture at large.

These are the conditions of belief under which we now live. This is the situation—a world in which the elites have declared that it is impossible and even dangerous to believe in God. This new event has provided the opening for the New Atheism. And what an opening it is.

TWO

The New Atheism and
the Assault on Theism

Having taken advantage of a cultural opening, the New Atheism has now emerged as a
potent challenge to Christianity. There are
four figures who have especially come to embody the
New Atheist movement. Indeed, one might call them
"The Four Horsemen of the New Atheist Apocalypse"—
Richard Dawkins, Daniel Dennett, Sam Harris, and
Christopher Hitchens. In order to respond effectively to
this new challenge, it is crucial that we as Christians
be at least conversant with these men and what they
are about.

Richard Dawkins holds the Charles Simonyi chair
for the Public Understanding of Science at Oxford
University, a chair that was established with a massive endowment in order to lure him back from the
University of California at Berkley, where he taught
after receiving his doctor of philosophy degree from
Oxford University. Born in 1941 in Kenya to a rather

well-established British family, he moved back to Great Britain when he was about eight years old. He attended school in Great Britain and then enrolled in Balliol College, Oxford, from which he received his undergraduate degree in zoology. In 1966, he received the doctorate from Oxford and then went almost immediately to the University of California at Berkeley to begin teaching. Eventually Oxford managed to lure him back, and he now holds one of the most famous—and well-funded—chairs in the entire university. He has also become probably the most recognizable scientist in the world.

In 1976 Dawkins wrote the book that established his mass reputation. Entitled *The Selfish Gene*, the book explained the particular facet of evolutionary theory for which Richard Dawkins is now famous.[1] His argument is that the basic unit of natural selection is the gene. Put in simplest form, Dawkins's theory is that genes are selfish, existing solely in order to replicate themselves, and as replicators they fuel the entire process of natural selection. This is the idea that gained for Dawkins such an immediate scientific reputation. As a matter of fact, at the high table of Darwinist theory, there are basically two rival understandings of the process of natural selection, and Dawkins's understanding of "the selfish gene" is quickly becoming the dominant one.

Dawkins did not write his book *The Selfish Gene* for

---

[1]Richard Dawkins, *The Selfish Gene* (Oxford: Oxford University Press, 1976).

the scientific community. He had already published his papers in peer-reviewed journals, and his research was well known in that community. He wrote the book for a mass audience because, even as he holds a chair for the public understanding of science, Richard Dawkins understands himself as an advocate, an evangelist of sorts, for evolutionary theory. He believes that an understanding of human evolution is absolutely essential to understanding where we are in the human story and how we should seize control of evolution as we look to the future. Dawkins also understands that evolution produces a worldview, and he believes that the worldview Darwinism produces is the only plausible worldview available to us. Now, this worldview obviously raises questions about the existence of God, questions which Dawkins says occurred to him as early as age nine, as he was being catechized. Reciting the questions and answers of his catechism, he realized that he did not believe these things, and he began to doubt.

In 1856, Charles Darwin wrote a letter to his friend Joseph Hooker in which he said, "What a book a devil's chaplain might write on the clumsy, wasteful, blunderingly low and horribly cruel works of nature."[2] Picking up on that line in that letter, Dawkins has declared himself the "Devil's Chaplain." He wrote a book by that title in 2003, dedicating it to his daughter Juliet, who

---

[2]Cited in Richard Dawkins, *A Devil's Chaplain: Reflections on Hope, Lies, Science, and Love* (New York: Houghton-Mifflin, 2003), 8.

was then ten. In that book Dawkins argues that evolution, in terms of its total understanding and its implications for the existence or nonexistence of God, should now be publicly discussed. In one essay included there, written originally in 1993 and entitled "Viruses of the Mind," Dawkins first spoke about the "virus of faith."[3]

At the end of *A Devil's Chaplain*, he addresses a letter to his ten-year-old daughter. Entitled "Good and Bad Reasons for Believing," the letter is a very interesting piece of parental advice. Dawkins suggests to his daughter three bad reasons to believe in any proposition or truth claim. The first of these is tradition.[4] This is especially important, he says, because children are "natural receptors of tradition," and therefore tradition is especially seductive to them. They find their identity as their parents tell them stories and as they find themselves situated within tradition. In fact, Dawkins points out to his daughter that the persistence of religious belief might be due to the fact that children "have to be suckers for traditional information, otherwise they do not survive."[5]

One of the other factors in Dawkins's thought here is a word he coined himself—"meme"—which refers to an intellectual unit similar to a gene that helps to explain the replication of thought.[6] Memes are sets of

[3]Ibid., 141.
[4]Ibid., 243.
[5]Ibid., 247.
[6]Dawkins, *The Selfish Gene*, 192.

ideas that are replicated in the society. Thus Dawkins is suggesting that parents pass "memes" on to their children just as they do genes. This Dawkins finds to be very dangerous and seductive.

Second, and equally perniciously, he suggests that another bad reason for believing is authority.[7] In other words, just because someone says something is true is no reason to believe that it is so. The third bad reason for believing, Dawkins suggests, is revelation, which he believes is categorically impossible.[8] Therefore, any claim of truth based upon any revelation, he suggests, should simply be dismissed out of hand. Seeing Dawkins's letter to his daughter, it is easy to understand how atheism would inevitably emerge.

In 2006 Dawkins wrote *The God Delusion*, the book that became his landmark bestseller, staying on the *New York Times*' list for several months.[9] Among the New Atheists, Dawkins is the most persistent, and he is probably also the best known and the most read.

* * *

The second of the New Atheists is Daniel Dennett, born in 1942 in Boston. A philosopher of mind and of science, Dennett has taught for almost his entire career at Tufts University, where he directs the Center for

---

[7]Dawkins, *Devil's Chaplain*, 244.
[8]Ibid., 245.
[9]Richard Dawkins, *The God Delusion* (New York: Houghton-Mifflin, 2006).

Cognitive Studies and is the Austin B. Fletcher Professor of Philosophy. He received his bachelor of arts from Harvard and his doctor of philosophy from Oxford one year prior to Dawkins's receiving the degree from the same university. Dennett's great life project is to prove that evolution alone explains human consciousness. There must be a wholly empirical understanding of human consciousness, he says, and he has gained considerable fame in the scientific community for his ideas. In 1992, much as Dawkins sought to popularize his thought with *The Selfish Gene*, Dennett sought to popularize his empirical understanding of human consciousness in a book entitled *Consciousness Explained*.[10] The book became one of those very rare science books that actually sells, and it gained a great deal of attention for the argument that human consciousness has to be reduced to a mechanistic and naturalistic understanding.

Like Dawkins, Dennett is absolutely committed to the worldview that evolution explains everything. In 1996 he published the book *Darwin's Dangerous Idea*, which comes down to this central point: Dennett recalls his experience as a boy interested in science, when he and a friend invented the idea of a "universal acid."[11] What if there existed an acid so powerful that it would dissolve anything, and therefore no container could be found that would safely contain it? What would hap-

[10]Daniel Dennett, *Consciousness Explained* (New York: Penguin, 1993).
[11]Daniel Dennett, *Darwin's Dangerous Idea* (New York: Simon and Schuster, 1996).

pen? Eventually, of course, the universal acid would destroy everything. Nothing would remain—a tantalizing thought to any schoolboy, and one that became a fuel for Dennett's intellectual development. When Dennett discovered Darwinism he believed that he had finally found the universal acid. His point is this: as an intellectual tool, Darwinism is just as corrosive and powerful as his hypothetical universal acid. It burns away everything. Put simply, once Darwinism is fully understood, every other truth claim will cease to hold power and cease to have credibility. Darwinism will be all that remains.

He says this: "Almost no one is indifferent to Darwin and no one should be. The Darwinian Theory is a scientific theory, and a great one, but that is not all that it is. The creationists who oppose it so bitterly are right about one thing: Darwin's dangerous idea cuts much deeper into the fabric of our most fundamental beliefs than many of its sophisticated apologists have yet admitted, even to themselves."[12] He's right, of course. If Darwinism is right, then there is no design in the universe and therefore no meaning, either. There is only Darwinism.

In 2006 Dennett wrote the book that establishes him as one of the four horsemen of the New Atheism, *Breaking the Spell: Religion as a Natural Phenomenon.*[13]

---

[12]Ibid., 18.
[13]Daniel Dennett, *Breaking the Spell: Religion as a Natural Phenomenon* (New York: Penguin, 2007).

The importance of this book lies in the fact that it presents religion in purely naturalistic terms. Even evolutionists need an argument that explains the persistence of religion. The basic problem is this: how do you explain religion? It's one thing to explain an appendage or an organ in a creature, but it's another thing to try to explain an idea as persistent as belief in God. So how does it happen? If the mind is nothing more than a chemical machine, a neurological machine developed for the process of evolution, then where did this (false) belief in a supernatural deity come from? Natural selection explains that those characteristics which confer some survival advantage are passed on, while those which do not eventually die out. Thus those creatures with larger brains have succeeded where those with smaller brains have not. Those who have the ability to walk have survived where those who had no such ability did not.

So why did those who believed in God survive while those who did not believe did not? If you hold to a purely natural understanding of religion like Dennett and Dawkins, there is really only one answer. You have to say that there must have been some evolutionary advantage at some point to believing in God. Somehow religious belief—and in particular belief in life-after-death, belief in God, belief in a supreme authority, belief in a revealed morality, and belief in a Divine Judge—somehow all this must produce replicators who replicate more successfully. Dennett's solution to this problem is to say that while belief in God must have conferred an evolutionary advantage somewhere back in time, it does so no longer. Thus, Dennett suggests, our great task in this generation is to rid ourselves of what was once an evolutionary advantage but is now an evolutionary disadvantage.

Another interesting thought to notice in Dennett is his creation of a new category that he calls "belief in belief." Dennett suggests that the persistence of belief in God is not all it is often thought to be, because if you scratch just beneath the surface, you find that fewer people believe in God than may first appear. Instead of believing in God, he says, they believe in *belief*. In other words, they have a functional understanding of religion. They really are not claiming cognitively to believe in God, because, as Dennett understands, if they really believed in God then they would have to live differently than they do. Israeli Prime Minister Golda Meir was once asked if she believed in God. Her response is a perfect example of belief in belief. "The Jews believe in God," she replied, "and I believe in the Jews." Dennett hopes that this "belief in belief" could be a way-station on the road to eventually being rid of belief in God altogether. Perhaps we are moving from belief in God to belief in *belief* and finally to no longer needing even *that* belief.

*   *   *

Sam Harris, born in 1967 to a Jewish mother and a
Quaker father, is roughly twenty years younger than
either Dennett or Dawkins.[14] His rebellion against
any kind of theistic belief began in his early adolescence when he refused to be bar mitzvahed.[15] He
attended Stanford University but dropped out after a
fairly unexplained incident with the drug Ecstasy.[16]
Around the same time, Harris had some sort of deeply
religious experience. Later he returned to Stanford
University to pursue his doctor of philosophy in neu-
roscience. Harris claims that he is under persistent
death threats from evangelical Christians, and thus
he can't release any personal information about himself. For that reason neither he, nor his publisher, nor
anyone else is very clear about many of the particu-
lars of his life.

What is clear, however, are the sales figures for his
books. Harris's 2004 book, *The End of Faith*, became
one of the bestsellers of that year, and it remains even
now among the top-ranked books sold at sites such as
Amazon.com.[17] The book is a broadside attack on theism, and it comes with incredible vitriol. Harris suggests that belief in God is inherently evil, beginning in

[14]David Segal, "Atheist Evangelist," *Washington Post*, October 26, 2006.
[15]Lisa Miller, "Beliefwatch: The Atheist," *Newsweek*, October 30, 2006.
[16]Segal, "Atheist Evangelist."
[17]Sam Harris, *The End of Faith* (New York: Norton, 2004).

evil mental and spiritual impulses and leading finally to evil social effects. God himself is an ogre, Harris says—especially the God of the Bible, who is not a god that any sane or morally sensitive person would believe in, much less love. Belief in God, Harris declares, corrupts human beings.

He writes, "Religious faith represents so uncompromising a misuse of the power of our minds that it forms a kind of perverse, cultural singularity."[18] In other words, it is "a vanishing point beyond which rational discourse proves impossible. When foisted upon each generation anew, it renders us incapable of realizing just how much of our world has been unnecessarily ceded to a dark and barbarous past."[19] As Harris sees it, we have deluded ourselves into thinking that religion is not that much of a threat. We have allowed it to persist as a "private matter" when we ought to have recognized it as a public danger.

One of the reasons Harris sees belief as so dangerous is that it makes persons self-centered. To believe that God cares about you as an individual, Harris would say, makes you a narcissist. To believe that God would have a personal relationship with you is self-centered in the extreme, and it inevitably leads to great selfishness because you then take great delight in this personal relationship with God that you imagine yourself to

---

[18]Ibid., 25.
[19]Ibid.

have. Not only so, but you also probably develop some sense of superiority over those who do not share this personal relationship and this personal knowledge. The fact that you believe that God cares about *you*, Harris would argue, says everything about you and nothing at all about God.

Evidently Harris did not think his first book was sufficient. Having sold *The End of Faith* by the hundreds of thousands, he wrote a second book in 2006 entitled *Letter to a Christian Nation*.[20] This very short book is supposedly addressed to conservative Christians, but if you read it believing that Harris is actually trying to speak to conservative Christians, you are missing the point. Like Dawkins and Dennett, Harris is really trying to reach a cultural elite. As he says himself, he wants to embolden secularists to make secularist claims more fearlessly in the public square. Though he casts the book in terms of a letter to Christian believers, it is actually a pep-talk intended for secularists. "The primary purpose of the book," Harris writes, "is to arm secularists in our society, who believe that religion should be kept out of public policy, against their opponents on the Christian right."[21]

This is not unique to Sam Harris. All of these writers to some extent—and Sam Harris to the greatest extent, perhaps—are really trying to embolden fellow secular-

---

[20]Sam Harris, *Letter to a Christian Nation* (New York: Knopf, 2006).
[21]Ibid., viii.

ists. They are trying to make secularism more mainstream. Last year an atheist group launched a hunt for the highest ranking atheist official in America. After much searching, they finally found Representative Pete Stark of California who, unfortunately for their movement, was not able to explain very well when the microphone was put in front of him *why* he didn't believe in God. Nonetheless he identified himself as a skeptic and unbeliever. It was a minor victory for organized atheism, but then again, after a nationwide search they could find only one member of Congress. Evidently, as Sam Harris says, identifying yourself as an atheist does not make for electoral success.

That raises another theme in Harris's writing. Harris addresses himself particularly to the United States, because he thinks the United States should be horribly embarrassed among the nations because we are not playing along with the secularization game. We have not followed Western Europe. This sense of embarrassment about the United States is a major preoccupation with Harris. He complains that, for some reason, a virulent stream of God-belief persists in this country, and that must be because of some basic fault in the American mind. As a matter of fact, Harris admits that he is scared by the fact that Americans tend to have such a low view of atheists. He cites studies showing that Americans don't trust atheists, and then concludes that it is simply not *safe* to be an atheist.

Of course the same is not true in Europe, and it has not been true for several decades. During the twentieth century, for instance, French President Francois Mitterrand was very publicly an atheist; indeed he had declared himself as such for all of his adult life. One book written about Mitterrand after his death was even entitled *Dying Without God*.[22] So, that long ago, Mitterrand's atheism was considered uneventful in France, which after the French Revolution had become deeply anticlerical and marked by a strong atheistic strain.

* * *

The fourth horseman of the New Atheist apocalypse is Christopher Hitchens. Born in 1949, Hitchens is a contrarian by self-description and an intellectual author, pundit, commentator, and critic. He is the brother, interestingly enough, of Peter Hitchens, a Christian believer who is also a pundit, commentator, and media personality. Estranged for a number of years, Peter and Christopher have since reconciled at some personal level. Christopher Hitchens is well known, even among those who have little interest in his atheism, for a radical political transition in his life. Early on he was a Trotskyite Marxist of the far Left. The events of September 11, 2001, however, moved him considerably to the right, at least in matters of foreign

---

[22]Franz-Olivier Giesbert, *Dying Without God* (New York: Arcade, 1998).

policy. He now believes that the threat of militant Islam is one of the world's great dangers and that it must be confronted head-on. Not incidentally, this all contributes heavily to his belief that *any* belief in God is a fundamental threat to civilization.

In 2007 Hitchens wrote his book entitled *God Is Not Great: How Religion Poisons Everything.*[23] In the book he speaks of his own Anglican boyhood, and much like Richard Dawkins, says that it was during his Anglican education that he began to doubt—and at about the same age. There is something to be learned here. A tepid introduction to Christianity turns out to be a poor preparation for life, and an even poorer preparation for hearing the gospel. The kind of institutionalized, "almost" Christianity that characterized much of British public school education is exactly what produced a Dawkins and a Hitchens.

Hitchens suggests that he has four irreducible objections to religious faith: first, it wholly misrepresents the origins of man and the cosmos. Second, he says, religion manages to combine the maximum of servility with the maximum of solipsism. Believers are servile in mind, he charges, and completely self-referential when it comes to truth. Third, he says, religion is a great cause of sexual repression. And fourth, religion is ultimately grounded in wishful thinking.[24]

---

[23]Christopher Hitchens, *God Is Not Great: How Religion Poisons Everything* (New York: Twelve, 2007).
[24]Ibid., 4.

From that ground, Hitchens attempts to shame persons into acknowledging their unbelief. Like the others, he is not necessarily trying to convince believers that they ought to abandon belief. He is seeking to create cultural momentum, to encourage others to be more vocal in their unbelief.

* * *

Considering the works of these four writers together, along with others like Michael Onfray in France and A. C. Grayling in Great Britain, we can identify eight hallmarks of the New Atheism—eight characteristics that set it apart from older forms of atheism and that frame its challenge to Christian belief.

First, the New Atheism is marked by an unprecedented new boldness. As we have already seen, in the older atheism there was usually some sense of longing and even a tragic sense of loss. Bertrand Russell, in his now infamous book *Why I Am Not a Christian*, betrayed some wistfulness, some sense that something important had been lost.[25] That sense of loss is completely missing in the New Atheism. The New Atheism is all about being rid of any pretension that anything important has been lost, and instead of requiem there is celebration! Even more, there is a shaming of those who claim to believe in God but actually do not. Recalling Daniel

---

[25]Bertrand Russell, *Why I Am Not a Christian* (Girard, KS: Haldeman-Julius, 1929).

Dennett's important distinction between belief in God and belief in belief, all four of these writers hope it might be possible to convince some persons who believe in *belief* that they instead should see belief in God as dangerous, and thus reverse their public posture. There is a new boldness, a direct attack on what they see as the pretensions of theism.

Second, there is a clear and specific rejection of the Christian God of the Bible. Twentieth-century atheists generally addressed themselves to the philosophical idea of a supernatural being or to the evil of a God who does not prevent moral evil. Whether it was Logical Positivism or some later variant of postmodernism, the suggestion was that "god" is an untenable *idea*. With the New Atheists, the argument is that what the Bible presents is an untenable *God*. The New Atheists acknowledge that the God of the Bible can be fairly well known, that he has (according to his believers) spoken in a book and defined himself. But building upon the thought of the protest atheists in the twentieth century, who rejected belief in any God in the wake of the Holocaust, the New Atheists go further to declare that it is now *evil* to believe in God—specifically, in the God of the Bible.

If the God of the Bible is Creator, they say, then he must, as B. B. Warfield insisted, take responsibility for his creation. And if he must take responsibility for his creation, then he has *much* to take responsibility for. If you read the Bible, say the New Atheists, you cannot avoid the conclusion that the majority of human beings who ever lived are going to be in eternal torment in hell. By any measure, they argue, such a God is an evil God, and those who would believe in such a God are themselves evil. This point is illustrated by philosopher David Lewis, who taught for many years at Princeton University. In an essay published after he died in 2001, Professor Lewis wrote: "Many Christians appear to be good people, people worthy of the admiration of those of us who are non-Christians. From now on let us suppose, for simplicity's sake, that these Christians accept a God who perpetrates divine evil, one who inflicts infinite torment on those who do not accept him. Appearances notwithstanding, are those who accept the perpetrator of divine evil themselves evil?"[26]

Third, the New Atheists explicitly reject Jesus Christ. Now this, too, is rather new, especially in its intensity. Reaching even as far back as the Gnostics and Marcion, many have suggested that the Old Testament presents a vengeful Creator God, whereas the New Testament presents a liberating, wonderful, incarnate, loving, self-sacrificial, tender savior: Jesus. The New Atheist will have none of that. Christopher Hitchens, for example, says that while the God of the Old Testament killed a lot of people, the book of Revelation presents

[26]David Lewis, "Divine Evil," *Philosophers without Gods: Meditations on Atheism and the Secular Life,* ed. Louise M. Antony (New York: Oxford University Press, 2007), 238.

Jesus as far more vengeful than even he. When it comes to violence, Hitchens would argue, Jesus makes the God of the Old Testament look like an amateur.[27] Sam Harris adds that even in the four Gospels, Jesus clearly believes that people are going to hell. Not only that, but in the book of Matthew, Jesus takes responsibility for the entire Old Testament—"not an iota, not a dot, will pass," he says (Matt. 5:18). He is not, as some Protestant liberals would have it, a new face of God, or a way for God to repair a bad reputation. No, Jesus is to be rejected just as forcefully as the vengeful God of the Old Testament.

For Richard Dawkins, the central evil of Jesus is restrictivism.[28] In other words, Dawkins argues that religion poses a social danger because it creates an "in" group and an "out" group, which is the very definition of exclusivism. Thus there are those who believe and those who reject, and the result is a fixed set of tribal identities that eventually become dangerous. In India, for example, there is continuing strife between Hindu believers and Muslim believers. Any kind of restrictivist or exclusivist truth claim, Dawkins says, will have this problem. And of course Jesus is no better, according to the New Atheists. His language in the Gospels is just as exclusivistic as the language of Israel in the Old Testament. Jesus speaks of his people in distinction to

---

[27]Hitchens, *God Is Not Great*, 109–22.
[28]Dawkins, *The God Delusion*, 293.

other people, of those who believe in him in contrast to those who do not.

Now the upshot of all this—the concern about "in" groups and "out" groups, together with the rejection of biblical theism—is that the whole idea of monotheism becomes a major problem. Stuart Hampshire, a philosopher at Princeton University, argued that monotheism is the great danger to humanity.[29] Similar arguments have been made by other figures in the intellectual culture. Novelist Gore Vidal, for example, says that monotheists believe in an evil "sky god" who calls them to do evil things in his name. What we face here is not a rejection of banal spirituality or merely of the etiquette of Victorian religion. This is a rejection, specifically, of theism and of monotheism—a rejection of the specific truth claims concerning the triune God of the Bible.

Fourth, the New Atheism is specifically grounded in scientific argument. Three of the four horsemen of the New Atheism are scientists by training, and Hitchens considers himself a person who is scientifically informed. Dennett, Dawkins, and Harris are explicitly committed to science, and even more—to scient*ism*. All three of them believe that science must, in the end, explain everything that is explicable. Their commitment to the worldview of naturalism and materialism is absolute and nonnegotiable. The greatest proof of

---

[29]Stuart Hampshire, *Justice Is Conflict* (Princeton: Princeton University Press, 2000), 51–75.

this, perhaps, is the research project to which Dennett has given his life, the quest to identify a purely physical understanding of human consciousness. Now that is truly a daunting challenge. Dennett will have to come up with a purely materialist interpretation of absolutely *everything*—from a mother's love for her child to voting patterns in a national election to, of course, belief in God. Every single emotive state, every single choice, every single action of the mind, every single artifact of consciousness must be explained in terms of chemicals interacting in the tissues of the brain.

The argument of the New Atheists is that science is the way of liberation, the way of freedom, and the way of enlightenment. So Richard Dawkins believes that evolutionary science is *the* means of enlightenment and the route to human liberation. Daniel Dennett believes that Darwinism is the universal acid that burns away everything, leaving nothing but itself as a causal explanation. Sam Harris believes that science holds the promise of a new human future, and he holds Christians responsible for holding up the scientific advances (such as embryonic stem-cell research) that could bring about this new human era. Not only so, but all of them are positively terrified by the fact that the majority of Americans do not believe in evolution.

One of the journalists who is very much a part of this conversation is Nicholas Kristof of the *New York Times*. Kristof does not himself despise evangelicals, though he's made very clear that he reserves the right to oppose all of evangelicalism's "despicable" public policy positions. Several years ago, Kristof wrote a column in which he marveled at and lamented the fact that more people in North America say they believe in the virgin birth of Christ than in evolution. The article goes on, of course, attempting to debunk the virgin birth of Christ and to argue that all intelligent, right-minded persons must accept the doctrine of evolution.[30] And yet, despite it all, the vast majority of Americans still reject evolution. For the New Atheists, that is a source of deep and unending frustration.

Fifth, the New Atheism is new in its refusal to tolerate moderate and liberal forms of belief. Now this something that is genuinely helpful. Unlike older forms of atheism, the New Atheists are not seeking to incite accommodationist forms of theistic belief. One of the great projects of twentieth-century theological liberalism was to save Christianity by accommodating it to the new cultural zeitgeist. Thus all the super-natural elements of traditional Christianity—miracles, verbal inspiration, resurrection—were quickly tossed out. Secularists assumed that this meant things were going their way. After all, *Time* magazine ran a cover story in the 1960s on the death of God.[31] Moreover, enormous changes were taking place in the mainline

---

[30]Nicholas Kristof, "Believe It, Or Not," *New York Times*, August 15, 2003.
[31]"Is God Dead?" *Time*, April 8, 1966.

Protestant denominations, with one theologian after another adopting accommodationist forms of theism. It looked like things were going the right way, and atheists and secularists very publicly encouraged these new, moderate forms of Christianity.

But no more. The New Atheists no longer see moderate and liberal forms of belief as societal goods, but rather as social evils. Of course moderate believers are not going to fly airplanes into skyscrapers, they would admit, nor will they try to control your sex life the way evangelical Christians supposedly will. But they are still dangerous because they're giving cover to the true "God-believers." They are making it more socially acceptable to believe. In the eyes of the New Atheists, moderate Christians are not part of the solution. They are part of the problem. They may think their accommodations with modernity have taken the sting out of Christianity and the threat out of their belief system, but the reality is that they are just enabling the fundamentalists—the real believers—because they are able to fly under the radar, covered by the moderates' popularity and tolerance.

Now why would all this be in any way helpful? The answer is because it reminds us that accommodationist theism gets one nowhere. It impresses no one. The denial of biblical theism is a failed intellectual project, not only because it denies the God of the Bible, but also because it does not even accomplish pragmatically what its proponents hoped it would accomplish. In the new intellectual climate in which we now find ourselves, an accommodated form of theism is no more acceptable to the cultural elites than a robust biblical faith.

The sixth distinction of the New Atheism is the attack on toleration. The American experiment of freedom of expression is considered by many of the New Atheists to be simply too dangerous, because it legitimizes the kinds of belief systems that are dangerous, and it does not distinguish between safe and unsafe forms of religion. Thus Sam Harris, more pointedly than the others, says that the time has come to rid ourselves of religious toleration, for it is an experiment that has become too expensive.[32]

Seventh, the New Atheists have begun to question the right of parents to inculcate belief in their own children. The accusation, most specifically from Dawkins, is that this is a form of child abuse. Now this is a very dangerous argument, because it is almost perfectly framed, politically speaking, in terms of the rights of the child and in terms of what possible harms might come to a child. Furthermore, in a day in which the functions of the family and the functions of parenthood are being stripped away by a bureaucratic society and a regulatory state, it is very tempting to the secularist Left to think that it might be possible to define the child as a unit unto himself. When that happens, when the

---

[32]Harris, *Letter to a Christian Nation*, xii.

child is identified as a self-defined unit apart from his or her parents, it is not difficult to arrive at the conclusion that the parents' prejudicing of the child in terms of religion is a form of child abuse.

John Dewey argued in this vein in the early twentieth century, suggesting that the only way to forge a common democratic culture was to separate the children of immigrants from the prejudices of their parents. And thus began the common school project to which he was so committed. So far as I know, however, Dewey never called it child abuse. That is a term that is unique to the New Atheists.

Eighth and finally, the New Atheists argue that religion itself must be eliminated in order to preserve human freedom. Freedom is the one great good for these secularists, and thus any restriction on human freedom is by definition wrong. In their view, humanity can never be free if the authority of God and church are not overturned. Thus, there is a moral impulse behind their ambitions—as is true of all revolutionary movements. And make no mistake—the New Atheism *does* represent a revolution.

THREE

The New Atheism and
the Defense of Theism

The challenge of the New Atheism demands a Christian response at so many levels. At the intellectual level, the New Atheism presents Christian theology with the need for a sustained and credible defense of theism—and of Christian theism in particular. At the worldview level, including the pre-theological patterns of thought, the New Atheism demands a refutation of naturalism as the only avenue of legitimate knowledge. At the moral level, the New Atheism challenges Christian theologians to respond credibly, but not merely with the intellect. As the late Carl F. H. Henry reminded evangelicals, the world is looking for an evangelical demonstration of Christianity, not merely an intellectual defense. Finally, at the level of public policy, Christians must contend with the claim that raising children to be Christian believers is a form of child abuse, as well as with the larger claim by some that theism is just too dangerous to be tolerated.

Atheism is not a new challenge, but the New Atheists are perceived as presenting a new and powerful refutation of theism. Their challenge deserves and demands a cogent Christian response.

*   *   *

Just two years prior to the publication of Dawkins's *The God Delusion*, Oxford theologian Alister McGrath released *The Twilight of Atheism: The Rise and Fall of Disbelief in the Modern World*.[1] Looking at the expanse of modern history in Western cultures, McGrath pointed to two pivotal events as bracketing the rise and fall of atheism—the fall of the Bastille in 1789 and the fall of the Berlin Wall in 1989. These two events, argue McGrath, marked the historical boundaries of the "remarkable rise and subsequent decline of atheism."

McGrath's confidence in the fall of atheism as a potent worldview was rooted in his sense that the fall of the Soviet secular state and its empire marked a turning point in Western thought. Even as the French Revolution had asserted secularism in the wake of the Enlightenment and the Age of Revolution, the fall of Soviet communism marked the end game of state-mandated secularism.

The Twilight of Atheism is a stimulating book and

---

[1]Alister McGrath, *The Twilight of Atheism: The Rise and Fall of Disbelief in the Modern World* (New York: Doubleday, 2004).

an instructive analysis of the development of atheism as a worldview in the West. Even so, the book's title—released just two years before the New Atheism emerged in full force—can be seen as an example of very poor timing. But McGrath was not really arguing that atheism would disappear, only that atheism had failed in its project to render belief in God—and in Christian theism in particular—intellectually incredible.

Atheism, he argued, had failed to excite the public imagination and, in his view, did not face a future that is "especially distinguished or exciting."[2] Atheism is marked by moral seriousness, he acknowledged, and it should be recognized for offering legitimate concerns about institutional Christianity. Indeed, atheism may at times strengthen Christian theology by forcing the identification of bad arguments and the development of better intellectual defenses of the faith.

In the end, McGrath argued that "Western atheism now finds itself in something of a twilight zone. Once a worldview with a positive view of reality, it seems to have become a permanent pressure group, its defensive agenda dominated by concerns about limiting the growing political influence of religion."[3]

As for its future, "We will have to wait and see."[4] Well, as it turned out, not for long.

The year after the publication of *The God Delusion*,

---

[2]Ibid., 272.
[3]Ibid., 279.
[4]Ibid.

McGrath and his wife, Joanna Collicutt McGrath, released *The Dawkins Delusion?: Atheist Fundamentalism and the Denial of the Divine.*[5] This new book was a direct response to Richard Dawkins who, according to the McGraths, had emerged after *The God Delusion* as "the world's most high-profile atheist polemicist."[6] Dawkins, they noted, "is out to convert his readers" and to reveal all theism as delusional.[7]

In 2005, McGrath had published *Dawkins' God: Genes, Memes, and the Meaning of Life.*[8] In this book, McGrath mentions that he had first come across Richard Dawkins's work in 1977 when he was completing his doctoral research in biochemistry at Oxford University. Thus, Dawkins was on McGrath's intellectual screen even before he established his reputation as "Darwin's Rottweiler." *Dawkins' God* is a calm and reasoned consideration of Dawkins's challenge to Christian theology. The book is particularly addressed to the worldview implications of Dawkins's naturalism and his extension of Darwinist theory into every dimension of culture and meaning. McGrath's main complaint is that Dawkins has misconstrued the relationship between science and religion. "Dawkins raises all the right questions," McGrath concedes, "and gives some interesting

[5]Alister McGrath and Joanna Collicutt McGrath, *The Dawkins Delusion: Atheist Fundamentalism and the Denial of the Divine* (Downers Grove, IL: InterVarsity, 2007).
[6]Ibid., 7.
[7]Ibid.
[8]Alister McGrath, *Dawkins' God: Genes, Memes, and the Meaning of Life* (Oxford: Blackwell, 2007).

answers."[9] Nevertheless, "they're not particularly reliable answers, admittedly, unless you happen to believe that religious people are science-hating fools who are into 'blind faith' and other unmentionable things in a big way."[10]

Alister McGrath would appear to be just the right figure to respond publicly to Dawkins. After all, McGrath is not only a theologian but an Oxford-educated scientist, holding a doctorate in molecular biophysics as well as a doctorate in theology. Furthermore, McGrath was once an atheist himself who had looked forward "to the demise of religion with a certain grim pleasure."[11] Joanna Collicutt McGrath is also a scientist specializing in clinical neuropsychology and the philosophy of religion.

Writing in the first person, McGrath points to the parallels and divergences between his trajectory and that of Richard Dawkins:

> Although I was passionately and totally persuaded of the truth and relevance of atheism as a young man, I subsequently found myself persuaded that Christianity was a much more interesting and intellectually exciting worldview than atheism. I've always valued free thinking and being able to rebel against the orthodoxies of an age. Yet I never expected where my free thinking would take me.

---

[9]Ibid., 158.
[10]Ibid.
[11]McGrath, *Delusion*, 8.

Dawkins and I have thus traveled in totally different directions, but for substantially the same reasons. We are both Oxford academics who love the natural sciences. Both of us believe passionately in evidence-based thinking and are critical of those who hold passionate beliefs for inadequate reasons. We would both like to think that we would change our minds about God if the evidence demanded it. Yet, on the basis of our experience and analysis of the same world, we have reached radically different conclusions about God.[12]

McGrath argues that Dawkins sees evolutionary science as "an intellectual superhighway to atheism."[13] Yet, these same sciences—and the intellectual habits they foster—led McGrath to the Christian faith.

At the first level, McGrath accuses Dawkins of writing a sloppy and unscientific book. "The book is often little more than an aggregation of convenient factoids suitably overstated to achieve maximum impact and loosely arranged to suggest that they constitute an argument."[14] *The God Delusion* is "half-baked nonsense" that is not intended to reach believers at all, McGrath asserts, because genuine believers will not even recognize their own beliefs in his presentation.[15] In other words, McGrath argues that Dawkins is really writing something of an inspirational work for his fel-

---

[12]Ibid., 9.
[13]Ibid.
[14]Ibid., 13.
[15]Ibid.

low atheists. If Dawkins really intended to reach believers with his arguments, he would be required first to come to a more adequate and respectful understanding of the beliefs he wishes believers to abandon.

In a steaming rebuke, McGrath argues that Richard Dawkins has become what he opposes—a fundamentalist without any openness to a critique of his own convictions and without any real desire to understand what he rejects.

The Dawkins Delusion is not a systematic refutation of *The God Delusion*. Instead, McGrath looks to several themes and points of argument in Dawkins's book and offers his own critique.

McGrath addresses Dawkins's argument that belief in God is basically infantile. With incalculable intellectual condescension, Richard Dawkins has suggested that those who believe in God are mired in an infantilism of the mind—an accusation he extends to cultures that would share or foster the same convictions. Even as Dawkins once urged humanity to "leave the crybaby stage and finally come of age," McGrath calls for Dawkins to give up his immature critique of theism.[16] After all, McGrath notes, the argument that belief in God is infantile can be instantly turned on its head. Theism is not irrational, but contrary to Dawkins, belief in God does not finally rest on any set of classical philosophical proofs. God is not "improbable" in any

---

[16]Ibid., 19.

sense greater than humanity itself is improbable on Dawkins's own terms—for Dawkins himself makes the point that the emergence of humanity is itself highly improbable.[17]

McGrath then moves to refute the claim made by Dawkins and others that science has somehow disproved God. As he explains, there can be no scientific determination of "ultimate questions."

> This means that the great questions of life (some of which are also scientific questions) cannot be answered with any degree of certainty. Any given set of observations can be explained by a number of theories. To use the jargon of the philosophy of science: Theories are under-determined by the evidence. The question then arises: What criteria can be used to decide between them, especially when they are "empirically equivalent"? Simplicity? Beauty? The debate rages, unresolved. And its outcome is entirely to be expected: The great questions remain unanswered. There can be no question of scientific "proof" of ultimate questions. Either we cannot answer them or we must answer them on grounds other than the sciences.[18]

This is not a refutation of the scientific method, McGrath asserts, but only a statement of its inherent limitations. Even as Dawkins suggests that real scientists *must* be

---

[17]Richard Dawkins, *Climbing Mount Improbable* (New York: Norton, 1996).
[18]McGrath, *Delusion*, 35.

atheists, McGrath argues that real scientists understand the limitations of the scientific method and would consider questions with an intellectual openness notably missing from Richard Dawkins. Dawkins sees the whole world divided into opposing camps of reason and superstition. McGrath sees this as yet another example of Dawkins's fundamentalism:

> Dawkins is clearly entrenched in his own peculiar version of a fundamentalist dualism. Yet many will feel that a reality check is appropriate, if not long overdue, here. Dawkins seems to view things from within a highly polarized worldview that is no less apocalyptic and warped than that of the religious fundamentalisms he wishes to eradicate. Is the solution to religious fundamentalism *really* for atheists to replicate its vices? We are offered an atheist fundamentalism that is as deeply flawed and skewed as its religious counterparts. There are better ways to deal with religious fundamentalism. Dawkins is part of the problem here, not its solution.[19]

The fact that Richard Dawkins makes his argument as a world-recognized scientist only serves to confuse the public about the intellectual credibility of his project in *The God Delusion*. In the end, Dawkins is writing in an area outside his expertise—a charge which is leveled by many other critics of his thought.

---

[19]Ibid., 48.

* * *

Another key aspect of Dawkins's atheism is his argument that religion originates in a need for consolation—an argument he shares with Daniel Dennett among others. But, as McGrath notes, this is hardly a new argument. It was classically put forward by Ludwig Feuerbach. McGrath reminds his readers that wanting something is not, in itself, any proof that the thing does not actually exist. He compares the human need for God to the powerful desire represented by thirst—and as thirst corresponds to the reality of water, so faith corresponds to the reality of God.

Given his worldview, Dawkins is led to offer an entirely naturalistic account of religious faith. His absolute and unbending commitment to naturalism as a worldview requires him to explain everything, from the smallest detail to the grandest theory, entirely in naturalistic terms. Accordingly, Dawkins argues that belief in God must once have served some evolutionary purpose, but it now represents a toxic "meme" that constantly replicates itself in the human brain.

Here, McGrath offers an incisive critique of Dawkins's claim that belief in God is a mere meme—a cognitive replicator passed from brain to brain. While McGrath does not refute the existence of memes—he even credits Dawkins with an intellectually stimulating idea—McGrath does insist that there is no evidence that memes even exist. The question of memes is not, McGrath insists, even a question of religion.

> It is whether the meme can be considered to be a viable scientific hypothesis when there is no clear operational definition of a meme, no testable model for how memes influence culture and why standard selection models are not adequate, a general tendency to ignore the sophisticated social science models of information transfer already in place, and a high degree of circularity in the explanation of the power of memes.[20]

Instead, a meme is basically "a biological notion" that is deeply rooted in Dawkins's evolutionary naturalism. Finally:

> Dawkins, in my view, makes his critique of religion dependent on a hypothetical, unobserved entity that can be dispensed with completely in order to make sense of what we observe. But isn't that actually a core atheist critique of God—that God is an unobserved hypothesis which can be dispensed with easily? The scientific evidence for memes is actually much weaker than the historical evidence for the existence of Jesus—something that Dawkins revealingly regards as an open question, while doggedly defending memes. And since the evidence for memes is so tenuous, do we have to propose a meme for believing in memes in the first place?[21]

---

[20]Ibid., 71–72.
[21]Ibid., 73–74.

McGrath's critique of Richard Dawkins is not limited to issues associated with science, for Dawkins himself does not limit himself to scientific concerns. One of Dawkins's central arguments is that faith in God is evil, leading believers to commit evil and violent acts.

McGrath acknowledges that believers of many forms have, indeed, committed great evil, but he insists that this is not *necessary* to religion. Thus, McGrath asserts that Dawkins has presented a one-sided view of history, selecting the evidence he believes is supportive of his case and ignoring all the rest. Like Dawkins, McGrath denounces the use of violence:

> Yet is this a *necessary* feature of religion? Here, I must insist that we abandon the outmoded idea that all religions say more or less the same things. They clearly do not. I write as a Christian who holds that the face, will, and character of God are fully disclosed in Jesus of Nazareth. And as Dawkins knows, Jesus of Nazareth did no violence to anyone. He was the object, not the agent, of violence. Instead of meeting violence with violence, rage with rage, Christians are asked to "turn the other cheek" and not to let the sun go down on their anger. This is about the elimination of the roots of violence—no, more than that: it is about its *transfiguration*.[22]

Furthermore, McGrath accuses Dawkins of failing to concede that when secularism is absolutized, it turns

---

[22]Ibid., 76.

to a violence well documented even in our own times. Dawkins, he asserts, "fails to appreciate that when a society rejects the idea of God, it tends to transcendentalize alternatives—such as the ideals of liberty or equality."[23] When this happens, these ideological alternatives become "quasi-authorities" that function much like religious doctrines.[24]

McGrath's critique of Dawkins—and beyond Dawkins to the project of the New Atheism—is worthy of careful consideration. In the end, however, McGrath's critique is most valuable for his incisive refutation and undermining of many of Dawkins's most central arguments. McGrath does not proceed to defend any particular model of theism. His response to Dawkins is primarily defensive and evaluative, even if richly analytical.

Another point of concern with McGrath's critique is the extent to which he accepts so much of the evolutionary theory that is central to Dawkins's own project. It seems that one of McGrath's central concerns is to accept the larger system of evolutionary thought while insisting that evolution does not *require* the rejection of theism. This argument comes with its own very significant limitations.

*　*　*

A similar approach is undertaken by another of Dawkins's most public critics. Alvin Plantinga, per-

---

[23]Ibid., 81.
[24]Ibid.

haps the most influential Christian philosopher in the world today, serves as John A. O'Brien Professor of Philosophy at the University of Notre Dame. After teaching for two decades at Calvin College, Plantinga moved to the faculty at the University of Notre Dame, where he has shaped a generation of Christian philosophers. Plantinga, like McGrath, does not oppose evolutionary theory per se, but suggests that Dawkins has taken naturalism to an absurd conclusion.

Plantinga's critique of Dawkins appeared in a review essay published in the February 2007 edition of *Books & Culture*.[25] In his review of *The God Delusion*, Plantinga minces no words. He identifies the book as "an extended diatribe against religion in general and belief in God in particular."[26] Plantinga identifies Richard Dawkins and Daniel Dennett as "the touchdown twins of current academic atheism" and addresses his critique to the entire movement.[27]

Like McGrath, Plantinga acknowledges the stature of Richard Dawkins as a research scientist and writer. Indeed, he identifies Dawkins as "perhaps the world's most popular science writer" and "a very gifted writer."[28] Yet, Plantinga insists that *The God Delusion* actually contains very little science and is mostly about philosophy and theology, "along with a substantial dash

---

[25]Alvin Plantinga, "The Dawkins Confusion," *Books & Culture*, February 2007, http://www.christianity today.com/bc/2007/002/1.21.html.
[26]Ibid., 1.
[27]Ibid.
[28]Ibid.

of social commentary decrying religion and its allegedly baneful effects."[29]

In one sense, Plantinga writes as a calm academic reviewing the work of another academic who has, perhaps temporarily, lost his sense of academic decorum and scholarship. Plantinga decries Dawkins for "the proportion of insult, ridicule, mockery, spleen, and vitriol" that is found in *The God Delusion*.[30] Indeed, Plantinga goes so far as to suggest that Dawkins could face a promising future as a writer of attack ads for politicians.

The central thrust of Plantinga's critique is directed to Dawkins's failure to demonstrate even a basic understanding of the philosophical and theological issues involved in theism. In unusually acerbic prose, Plantinga suggests: "Why, you might say that some of his forays into philosophy are at best sophomoric, but that will be unfair to sophomores; the fact is (grade inflation aside), many of his arguments would receive a failing grade in a sophomore philosophy class."[31] Plantinga admits his own irritation in reading the book, and he almost suggests that the book is so philosophically vacuous as to be unworthy of serious consideration. Nevertheless, given the *public* significance of the work, Plantinga proceeds to take a closer look at Dawkins's proposals.

Plantinga takes a particular look at Dawkins's

---

[29]Ibid.
[30]Ibid.
[31]Ibid., 1–2.

suggestion that God must not exist because the very idea of God's existence is "monumentally improbable." The improbability of God's existence, Dawkins insists, is due to the fact that if he is indeed God, he must be highly *complex*. Given Dawkins's understanding of evolutionary theory, and perfectly consistent with his naturalistic worldview, he holds that something which is highly complex is also highly improbable.

Plantinga, who understands theism in both philosophical and theological terms, argues that Dawkins has committed a huge category error at this point. There is absolutely no reason to believe that God is *complex* in the sense that Dawkins insists he must be. Dawkins's evolutionary worldview leaves absolutely no room for any design or designer, but Plantinga suggests that in this case Dawkins is merely taking naturalism to an absurd conclusion. Here is the core of Plantinga's case against Dawkins:

> So first, it is far from obvious that God is complex. But second, suppose we concede, at least for purposes of argument, that God *is* complex. Perhaps we think the more a being knows, the more complex it is; God, being omniscient, would then be highly complex. Perhaps so; still, why does Dawkins think it follows that God would be improbable? Given *materialism* and the idea that the ultimate objects in our universe are the elementary particles of physics, perhaps a being that knew a great deal would be improbable—

how could those particles get arranged in such a way as to constitute a being with all that knowledge? Of course we aren't *given* materialism. Dawkins is arguing that theism is improbable; it would be dialectically deficient *in excelsis* to argue this by appealing to materialism as a premise. *Of course* it is unlikely that there is such a person as God if materialism is true; in fact materialism logically entails that there is no such person as God; but it would be obviously question-begging to argue that theism is improbable because materialism is true.[32]

In the end, Plantinga rightly identifies the central problem as Dawkins's naturalism. Given his absolute and uncritical acceptance of naturalism as a worldview, Dawkins is left with nothing but materialism, and his own lack of intellectual humility is seen in the fact that he simply assumes that his own worldview is the only *possible* or *credible* worldview in the modern age. But as Plantinga explains, it is naturalism itself which is finally self-refuting:

From a theistic point of view, we'd expect that our cognitive faculties would be (for the most part, and given certain qualifications and caveats) reliable. God has created us in his image, and an important part of our image bearing is our resembling him in being able to form true beliefs and achieve knowledge. But from a naturalist point of view the thought

---

[32]Ibid., 4.

that our cognitive faculties are reliable (produce a preponderance of true beliefs) would be at best a naïve hope. The naturalist . . . [would] have to hold that it is unlikely, given unguided evolution, that we live in a sort of dream world as that we actually know something about ourselves and our world. . . .

The real problem here, obviously, is Dawkins's naturalism, his belief that there is no such person as God or anyone like God. That is because naturalism implies that evolution is unguided. So a broader conclusion is that one can't rationally accept both naturalism and evolution; naturalism, therefore, is in conflict with a premier doctrine of contemporary science. People like Dawkins hold that there is a conflict between science and religion because they think there is a conflict between evolution and theism; the truth of the matter, however, is that the conflict is between science and *naturalism*, not between science and belief in God.[33]

Plantinga asserts that Dawkins's work and the naturalism associated with the New Atheism do not even come close to refuting belief in God and establishing that theistic beliefs are mistaken or delusional. Instead, "the naturalism that Dawkins embraces . . . in addition to its intrinsic unloveliness and its dispiriting conclusions about human beings and their place in the universe, is in deep self-referential trouble. There

---

[33]Ibid., 7–8.

is no reason to believe it; and there is excellent reason to reject it."[34]

* * *

The critiques offered by Alister McGrath and Alvin Plantinga are instructive. In both cases, Richard Dawkins is seen as the most formidable of the figures associated with the New Atheism. The popularity of *The God Delusion* and many of Dawkins's other titles has established him as the New Atheist of most central concern. It is telling that both McGrath and Plantinga identify Dawkins in this way even as they come from different academic disciplines.

At the same time, there are inherent limitations in the approach undertaken by both of these figures. McGrath and Plantinga offer what is essentially a negative critique of the New Atheism. In both cases, the critique is intellectually devastating. McGrath reveals the fact that Dawkins misconstrues the relationship between science and religion and in so doing fails to demonstrate the kind of scientific credibility and openness that marks authentic scientific inquiry. Plantinga, on the other hand, reveals Dawkins to be philosophically irresponsible, failing to understand what a college sophomore should know in terms of philosophy and argumentation. Dawkins, Plantinga explains, "seems

---

[34]Ibid., 8.

to have chosen God as his sworn enemy."[35] With God as his enemy, Dawkins simply resorts to diatribe and reckless argument in order to press his case.

On the basis of their critiques, it would seem fair to believe that both McGrath and Plantinga would extend their critiques from a focus on Richard Dawkins to the larger project of the New Atheism. Indeed, both make mention of Daniel Dennett, and Alvin Plantinga identifies Sam Harris as a "junior partner" in the enterprise of the New Atheism.

In some sense, the Achilles heel of the critiques offered by McGrath and Plantinga might be their own acceptance of the larger project of evolution. On this ground, it seems entirely possible that Richard Dawkins, Daniel Dennett, and Sam Harris could simply return the favor and accuse McGrath and Plantinga of failing to take the theory of evolution to its necessary conclusion—naturalism.

In the end, evangelical Christians must remember that the burden of our concern is not merely to refute atheism or to argue for the intellectual credibility of theism in any generic or minimal form. Instead, our task is to present, to teach, to explain, and to defend *Christian* theism. On this point, the defense of biblical theism reveals the great divide in intellectual thought to be not merely over the *existence* of God but over the question of whether he has *spoken*. The materialism

---

[35]Ibid., 1.

and naturalism that are so central to the New Atheism simply reject the category of revelation out of hand. This, in the end, is the real impasse. The issue is not merely metaphysics, but epistemology.

The credibility of Christian theology is thus essentially tied to the credibility of biblical revelation. The refutation of the New Atheism and the critiques offered on the basis of scientific theory and philosophy are helpful. But in the end, the self-authenticating character of divine revelation is the only ground upon which a distinctively *Christian* theism can be established.

FOUR

The New Atheism and
the Future of Christianity

There is now no question that the New Atheism will present a continuing challenge to Christianity in the twenty-first century. Given the highly public nature of this challenge, and the unique challenges posed by the New Atheism, as thoughtful Christians we must frame our thinking about the future with this reality in mind.

Of course, even as atheism has been an enduring challenge to theism, we are reminded that the word *atheist* was not necessary in the English language until the sixteenth century. Recent polls and surveys indicate that an increasing percentage of Americans are identifying as atheists or agnostics. It is still only a very small minority who identify themselves explicitly as atheists, but the number of Americans who identify with no particular faith is rising, and the public profile of atheism has become far more prominent with the rise of the New Atheism. In other words, atheism now appears to be far more of a legitimate cultural option than was the case even in the last years of the twentieth century.

Without doubt, the twenty-first century represents challenges to Christianity far beyond the New Atheism. Nevertheless, the New Atheism is itself a key illustration of the manifold theological challenges faced by the church in the postmodern age. As a matter of fact, the New Atheism—hard-wired to its own concept of scientific knowledge—is in some ways a refutation of the postmodern mood. The New Atheists are not relativists, and they do not believe that all truth is merely the product of social construction. To the contrary, the New Atheists dignify the truth question even as they oppose the truth most central to Christianity—the existence of the self-revealing God.

The failure of the dominant secularization theory, as we have noted, is revealed in the fact that the vast majority of Americans—and Europeans for that matter—continue to claim some form of religious identification. Especially in the United States, high rates of religious involvement and Christian identification continue to refute the older model of secularization that had predicted the evaporation of theistic faith in the face of modernity's new categories of thought and life. At the same time, the newer understanding of secularization represented by the theories of Charles Taylor, Peter Berger, and Robert Wuthnow[1] suggests

---

[1] See, e.g., Wuthnow, *After the Baby-Boomers*; *America and the Challenges of Religious Diversity*; *After Heaven: Spirituality in America Since the 1950s*; *The Restructuring of American Religion*.

that the process of secularization in the United States is best seen in the rise of "spirituality" as a replacement for identification with organized religion. Steve Bruce of the University of Aberdeen agrees that what secularization produced is not an absolute absence of religious forms, but rather the prevalence of a nontheistic form of belief. These nontheistic or vaguely-theistic forms of belief can range from the New Age movement to the various quests for spirituality that mark popular culture and fit personal taste.

* * *

Back in the 1960s, University of Chicago historian of religion Joseph M. Kitagawa distinguished primitive, classical, and modern forms of religion.[2] When defining "modern" religions, Kitagawa suggested that three factors distinguish the modern mode. Modern religions feature, first, a "preoccupation with the meaning of human existence"; second, a "this-worldly soteriology"; and third, "the search for 'freedom' rather than the preservation of 'order.' "[3]

In essence, Kitagawa argued that the collapse of the supernatural and the decline of authority would lead to a radical transformation of religion in the modern age.

---

[2]Joseph M. Kitagawa, "Primitive, Classical, and Modern Religions: A Perspective on Understanding the History of Religions," in *The History of Religions: Understanding Human Experience,* ed. J. M. Kitagawa (Atlanta: Scholars Press, 1987), 27–46.
[3]Ibid., 41.

In one sense, Kitagawa saw the postmodern age coming. The three factors he identified, though now somewhat anachronistic, are still recognizable within the context of the "changed conditions of belief" that now represent such a challenge to Christianity.

The New Atheists address themselves to these changed conditions of belief, with the strident denial of theism as the centerpiece of their argument. Among the New Atheists, Sam Harris seems to believe that a vague sort of Eastern spirituality is perfectly acceptable, even with the complete denial of theism. Richard Dawkins and Christopher Hitchens, on the other hand, demonstrate no respect whatsoever for the vague spirituality that is left when theism disappears. Daniel Dennett, we may surmise, would see these "spiritualities" as less dangerous than Christian theism.

In any event, the point of this review is to assert with clarity that the future of Christianity cannot be found in any accommodation to vague spirituality or to the New Atheism. Christians must summon the courage to respond to this challenge with the full measure of conviction and with a bold assertion of biblical theism.

* * *

At this point, it is instructive to note that some theologians have made very different proposals. Tina Beattie, vice president of the Catholic Theological

Society of Great Britain and a professor of theology at Roehampton University in London, has responded to the New Atheism with her recent book, *The New Atheists: The Twilight of Reason and the War on Religion.*[4] Beattie is a feminist as well as a Catholic theologian, and in her view the New Atheism is a "primarily British and American phenomenon."[5] Beattie sees the rise of the New Atheism as an opportunity to replace classical Christian theism with her own revisionist theology.

She describes the controversy over the New Atheism as a male-oriented debate. "I approach the New Atheism with different arguments than those offered by my male colleagues who have so far entered the fray," Beattie asserts.[6] She refers to the "testosterone-charged" nature of the debate and argues: "There is something a little comic, if not a little wearisome, about this perennial stag-fight between men of Big Ideas, with male theologians rushing to defend the same pitch that they have fought over for centuries, which is now being colonized by men of Science rather than men of God."[7]

Beattie recognizes that the New Atheists do present a challenge to Christian theology. Nevertheless, she bemoans the fact that the response to the New Atheists has come primarily from those prepared to defend biblical theism. In her words:

---

[4]Tina Beattie, *The New Atheists: The Twilight of Reason and the War on Religion* (Maryknoll, NY: Orbis, 2008).
[5]Ibid., 5.
[6]Ibid., 9.
[7]Ibid., 9–10.

> Those who have sought to present a more positive view of religion so far have tended to come from a fairly conservative Christian perspective. As a result, the debate is too narrowly focused on questions of rationality and belief, and it fails to take account of the many different challenges posed to both Western secularism and religious traditions by those whose voices are excluded from the conversation.[8]

Intending to transcend the argument, Beattie urges, "So let the men fight about God if they want to. My concern is not with debates about God but with creation and nature, with language and meaning, with people, and with kindness."[9]

In other words, Tina Beattie wants to replace Christian theism with a completely new theology, one that will reverse what she sees as the patriarchal structure of the classical Christian tradition and one that will dethrone authorities such as the Bible in terms of theological method.

It is instructive to look at her proposal precisely because she urges the Christian church to take a direction that others might see as less radical than it is. She simply agrees with many of the criticisms leveled at Christianity by the New Atheists but argues that Christianity can be reconstituted in a form that avoids these perceived errors.

---

[8]Ibid., 2.
[9]Ibid., 10.

Interestingly, Beattie understands the connection between the doctrine of creation and classical biblical theism. Thus, her radically revised theism is perfectly suited to embrace the evolutionary theory—indeed much of the naturalism—assumed as fundamental by the New Atheism. She is embarrassed that many of the Christian responses to the New Atheists have come from conservative Christians, and she, along with so many others, is particularly embarrassed by the continuing influence of Creationists. In fact, many liberal theologians seem to believe that Creationists (and included within this category are all who raise fundamental questions about evolutionary theory) are really to blame for the rise of the New Atheism. Given the scientism and naturalism that drives the New Atheists, this argument comes down to the fact that the Creationists have brought this war upon Christianity by insisting that evolution cannot account for the cosmos and that evolutionary theory is incompatible with biblical theism.

Beattie considers the assaults launched by Richard Dawkins and Christopher Hitchens upon Christianity to be driven by their animus toward the Christian Scriptures. In her view this is completely unnecessary. In this sense, she accuses Hitchens and Dawkins of making the same mistake made by fundamentalists—reading the Bible as if it is true. She suggests that a better place to start would be by "revisiting the Bible as fiction, but fiction worth reading."[10]

When Hitchens and Dawkins complain about the acts of God in the Old Testament, Beattie simply insists that these were never meant to be taken seriously anyway. The Old Testament books are "documents of inestimable historical and literary worth," she insists, "but their value has been all but destroyed for a modern generation of readers, because they carry the burden of divine revelation which demands that they be read as more than literature."[11] She agrees that the Old Testament includes "shocking stories of destruction and violence," and she repudiates "the repugnantly misogynistic tone" of some Old Testament writings.[12] She suggests that these stories should not be read as historical truth, much less as divine mandates, but rather that the narratives should be "read against the grain," in an undisguised form of literary deconstructionism.

Similarly, Beattie would reassure the New Atheists that in the New Testament, "we encounter neither the militarism nor the poetry of the Old Testament— with the exception of the vivid apocalyptic rhetoric of the Book of Revelation."[13] As she extends her argument, she assures her readers that "most educated

---

[10]Ibid., 82.
[11]Ibid., 81.
[12]Ibid., 82.
[13]Ibid., 83.

Christians are well aware of the contradictions, difficulties, and cultural anachronisms found in the New Testament."[14]

* * *

A similar approach is represented by *God and the New Atheism: A Critical Response to Dawkins, Harris, and Hitchens* by John F. Haught, senior fellow in science and religion at the Woodstock Theological Center at Georgetown University.[15] Haught has long been involved in the debate over the relation of theology to science. For thirty-five years, he served as chair of the Department of Theology at Georgetown University. His previous works include positive theological evaluations of Darwin and evolution. In *God and the New Atheism*, Haught, like Beattie, expresses regret that so much of the attention is given to the conflict between conservative Christians and the New Atheists.

Nevertheless, Haught's critique of the New Atheism is far more insightful and more interesting than that offered by Tina Beattie. He writes of the New Atheism with something like a sense of near exhaustion, seeing this new movement as, in the end, theologically uninteresting:

---

[14]Ibid.

[15]John F. Haught, *God and the New Atheism: A Critical Response to Dawkins, Harris, and Hitchens* (Louisville: Westminster, 2008).

I must confess, however, my disappointment in witnessing the recent surge of interest in atheism. It's not that my livelihood as a theologian is remotely at stake—although the authors in question would fervently wish that it were so. Nor is it that the treatment of religion in these tracts consists mostly of breezy overgeneralizations that leave out almost everything that theologians would want to highlight in their own contemporary discussion of God. Rather, the New Atheism is so theologically unchallenging. Its engagement with theology lies at about the same level of reflection on faith that one can find in contemporary creationist and fundamentalist literature. This is not surprising since it is from creationist and intelligent design theists that the New Atheists have garnered much of their understanding of religious faith. Mainline theologians, as well as students of intellectual history, will find in these publications very little that they have not seen before.[16]

Haught has already staked his theological reputation on the fact that there is no fundamental conflict between Darwin and Christian theology—at least the theology of liberal Protestantism and liberal Catholicism. At the most fundamental level, he rejects the central argument of Richard Dawkins and Daniel Dennett that "one must decide between theological and Darwinian explanations."[17]

---

[16]Ibid., xi.
[17]Ibid.

When Haught refers to "theology" he refers exclusively to those identified with the more liberal trajectory of twentieth-century theological thought, both Protestant and Roman Catholic. As he describes his theological method:

> By using the term "theological" here I mean to indicate, first of all, that my reflections arise out of my belonging to a theistic religious tradition, that is, one that professes belief in a personal God, a God of infinite power and love, who creates and sustains the world, and who forever opens up the world to a new and unprecedented future, a God who makes all things new. This essentially biblical understanding of God holds that the divine mystery can be approached only by way of faith, trust, and hope (which are almost indistinguishable concepts in biblical literature), not as a present cognitive or religious possession. Nevertheless, even though God cannot be known apart from faith and hope, most theology allows that faith and hope are entirely consistent with and fully supportive of human reason, including its pursuit of scientific understanding.[18]

The theologians Haught identifies as exemplars of his model of theology include Paul Tillich, Alfred North Whitehead, Paul Ricoeur, Rudolf Bultmann, Edward Schillebeeckx, Bernard Lonergan, Karl Barth, Karl Rahner, Jürgen Moltmann, Wolfhart Pannenberg,

---

[18]Ibid., xii.

Dorothee Sölle, and Sallie McFague, among others. To a greater or lesser extent, what marks the commonality among these thinkers is a rejection of classical theism and propositional revelation. What makes the list all the more interesting is that several of the figures listed among his favorite theologians are those who would reject Haught's own definition of theology—especially his insistence on belief in a personal God.

Like Beattie, Haught is convinced that the New Atheists have made the error of reading Christianity through the lens of conservative believers. Conservative Christians and the New Atheists make the mistake of thinking of faith "in a narrow intellectual and propositional sense."[19] This, he asserts, is no more than "echoing a now-obsolete theology."[20]

Like Alister McGrath, Haught also accuses Richard Dawkins, in particular, of falsely extending the scientific method to all areas of knowledge. He disapprovingly cites Dawkins's Tanner Lecture on Human Values delivered at Harvard University in 2003, where Dawkins stated: "It may be, that humanity will never reach the quietus of complete understanding, but if we do, I venture the confident prediction that it will be science, not religion, that brings us there. And if that sounds like scientism, so much the better for scientism."[21] In this sense, Haught comes very close

---

[19]Ibid., 5.
[20]Ibid.
[21]Ibid., 19.

to accusing Dawkins of a form of fundamentalism, the accusation central to McGrath's critique.

Like Alvin Plantinga, Haught suggests that the New Atheists lack a first-year student's knowledge of philosophy and theology. In one of the most interesting sections of his critique, Haught suggests that the New Atheists actually pale when measured against the more hard-line atheism represented by Albert Camus and Jean-Paul Sartre. Haught approvingly cites Sartre's remark that, "atheism is a cruel and long-range affair."[22] In essence, Haught argues that the New Atheists fail to take their own atheism with full seriousness. The older atheists, identified as the "more muscular critics of religion," were, according to Haught, "at least smart enough to realize that a full acceptance of the death of God would require an asceticism completely missing in the New Atheistic formulas."[23]

In the central portion of his book, Haught returns to his concern that the New Atheists have misunderstood Christian theology as a project. By identifying Christian theology with its more conservative forms, the New Atheists miss the fact that the theologians have begun to play a very different game.

For example, Haught, along with Beattie, is appalled by the identification of Christian theology with biblical literalism. "Both scientific and religious literalists share

---

[22]Ibid., 20.
[23]Ibid., 21.

the belief that there is nothing beneath the surface of the text they are reading—nature in the case of science, sacred Scriptures in the case of religion," Haught asserts.[24] Biblical literalism is the mirror error to scientism because "the religious literalist assumes that the full depth of what is going on in the real world is made evident to the true believer in the plainest sense of the sacred text."[25]

This analysis, perfectly consistent with the theological method he has articulated, allows Haught, like Beattie, to deconstruct the biblical text in order to remove those passages so offensive to the New Atheists. Christian theology, according to his definition, would avoid "the more typically creationist and historically anachronistic mentality" shared by both conservative Christians and the New Atheists. When Christopher Hitchens points to alleged discrepancies and contradictions in the biblical text, Haught is completely unmoved. Indeed, he alleges that Hitchens "shares with his extremist religious adversaries the assumption that grasping the full substance of biblical faith requires that the sacred text be taken literally."[26] According to Haught, "Most Christian scholars today delight in these factually irreconcilable accounts of Jesus' birth, since through them the two evangelists [Matthew and Luke] are able to introduce idiosyncratic theological

---

[24]Ibid., 30.
[25]Ibid.
[26]Ibid., 31.

themes that they carry through the remainder of their Gospels."[27]

It becomes clear that Haught is just as concerned about those he identifies as "extremist" believers as the New Atheists are. This means that Haught, with Beattie, is particularly appalled by those who would defend the historicity of the Genesis accounts of creation and, more broadly, those who would argue that evolutionary theory and biblical theism are fundamentally incompatible. Daniel Dennett, he argues, simply reads the Bible the same literalist way that Creationists do.

The New Atheists identify Christianity in terms of its "fundamentalists and fanatics,"[28] and thus misconstrue the postmodern shape of Christian faith. As Haught explains:

> The New Atheists, none of whom exhibit scholarly expertise in the field of religious studies, have methodically avoided theologians and biblical scholars as irrelevant to the kind of instruction their books are intended to provide. Instead, they have acquired their expertise in religious studies by limiting their research almost exclusively to the doctrinaire radicals and reactionaries about whom they are warning us. In order to grasp what religion really is, the atheists imply, all we need to focus on are its extremists, literalist interpreters, super-sectarians, inquisitors, and terrorists.[29]

---

[27]Ibid.
[28]Ibid., 36.
[29]Ibid.

When the New Atheists, and Sam Harris in particular,
argue that theology must be eliminated in every form,
Haught suggests that his argument "is comparable,
of course, to abolishing sex abuse by first abolishing
sex."[30]

By the time his book reaches its conclusion, Haught
does not call for a new conversation between Christian
theologians and the New Atheists. Instead, he simply
remarks that "the level of theological discernment by
the New Atheists is too shallow and inaccurate even to
begin such a conversation."[31]

* * *

When looking at these two liberal responses to the
New Atheism, we can detect a trajectory that is also
shared by some who are far less candid about their own
liberal convictions. In the end, Tina Beattie and John
Haught assist us in understanding that the accommodationist response to the New Atheism—and to the
larger challenge of modern thought—is simply not an
option. Evangelical Christians simply cannot surren-
der biblical authority, propositional revelation, and
biblical theism in order to meet the various challenges
presented to us in the twenty-first century.

Looking a bit closer at one particular aspect of the

---

[30]Ibid., 37.
[31]Ibid., 93.

liberal response is particularly instructive. One of the ironies of Haught's argument is that he affirms the existence of a personal God but also points to Paul Tillich as an exemplar of the theological method he endorses—the theological method completely missed, he argues, by the New Atheists. The irony in this is, of course, that Paul Tillich explicitly rejected the notion of a personal God. Indeed, Tillich argued that the very concept of a personal God was, in essence, a form of idolatry.

This illustration takes on an even greater significance in light of the fact that Tillich is also mentioned by the late Carl Sagan. Sagan, who died in 1996, was professor of astronomy and space sciences at Cornell University. Prior to the rise of Richard Dawkins, Sagan was almost surely the most famous scientist in the world, rivaled only perhaps by Stephen Hawking of Cambridge University. Sagan, like Dawkins, was a doctrinaire atheist. In 1985, Sagan was invited to give the famous Gifford Lectures in Scotland—a lectureship explicitly devoted to natural religion. In his lecture, Sagan defended his atheistic worldview, even as he suggested that theism was a largely incoherent concept. Most importantly, he argued that Paul Tillich served as an illustration of this confusion. In Sagan's words:

> And the subject is further confused by the fact that prominent theologians such as Paul Tillich, for example, who gave the Gifford Lectures many years ago,

explicitly denied God's existence, at least as a supernatural power. Well, if an esteemed theologian (and
he's by no means the only one) denies that God is
a supernatural being, the subject seems to me to
be somewhat confused. The range of hypotheses
that are seriously covered under the rubric "God" is
immense. A naïve Western view of God is an outsize,
light-skinned male with a long white beard, who sits
on a very large throne in the sky and tallies the fall
of every sparrow.[32]

The irony of Tillich's atheism is incredibly instructive. Writing over twenty-five years before Carl Sagan
delivered his Gifford Lectures, atheist philosopher
Sidney Hook of New York University published an essay,
"The Atheism of Paul Tillich."[33] Hook identified Tillich
as "one of the heroic figures of religious thought,"[34] but
he rooted Tillich's heroism in the fact that he, along
with other atheists, was willing to declare that the God
of classical Christianity is dead. In this case, Hook's
perspective as an avowed atheist is extremely helpful,
for we, along with Hook, must wonder in what sense
Tillich can be considered a theologian at all:

With amazing courage Tillich boldly says that the
God of the multitudes does not exist, and further,

[32]Carl Sagan, *The Varieties of Scientific Experience: A Personal View of the Search for God*, ed. Ann Druyan (New York: Penguin, 2006), 149.
[33]Sidney Hook, "The Atheism of Paul Tillich," in *Religious Experience and Truth: A Symposium*, ed. Sidney Hook (New York: New York University Press, 1961).
[34]Ibid., 59.

that to believe in His existence is to believe in an idol and ultimately to embrace superstition. God cannot be an entity among entities, even the highest. He is being-itself. In this sense Tillich's God is like the God of Spinoza and the God of Hegel. Both Spinoza and Hegel were denounced for their atheism by the theologians of the past, because their God was not a Being or an Entity. Tillich, however, is one of the foremost theologians of our time.[35]

All this brings to mind my favorite quotation from the late historian Eugene D. Genovese, himself an atheist, who wrote, "I intend no offense, but it takes one to know one. And when I read much Protestant theology and religious history today, I have the warm feeling that I am in the company of fellow nonbelievers."[36]

Thus, Tillich, along with Beattie and Haught, serves to remind us of a road Christian theology must not take. We simply cannot follow the programs offered by liberal theology and the theological revisionists. Theologians, including those who style themselves as evangelicals, who urge an accommodationist posture with modern secularism, present a prescription for theological disaster. The God who would be rendered acceptable to the secular age is a God who would bear no resemblance to the God of the Bible. This new God would be a God who cannot save.

---

[35]Ibid., 62.
[36]Eugene D. Genovese, *The Southern Front: History and Politics in the Cultural War* (Columbia, MO: University of Missouri Press, 1995), 9–10.

*   *   *

In conclusion, we must return to the point where
we began. It becomes clear that the New Atheism has
exploited an opening presented by significant changes
in prevailing patterns of thought. In this light, the contributions of Charles Taylor become especially helpful.
We must acknowledge that most educated persons liv-
ing in Western societies now inhabit a cultural space
in which the conditions of belief have been radically
changed. Whereas it was once impossible *not* to believe
and later *possible* not to believe, for millions of people
today, the default position is that it is impossible *to
believe*. The belief system referenced in this formula is
that of biblical theism—the larger superstructure of the
Christian faith.

In terms of our own evangelistic and apologetic
mandate, it is helpful to acknowledge that only a minority of those we seek to reach with the gospel are truly
and self-consciously identified with atheism in any
form. Nevertheless, the rise of the New Atheism presents a seductive alternative for those inclined now to
identify more publicly and self-consciously with organized nonbelief. The far larger challenge for most of us
is to communicate the gospel to persons whose minds
are more indirectly shaped by these changed conditions
of belief.

The greater seduction is towards the only vaguely

theistic forms of "spirituality" that have become the belief systems (however temporarily) of millions. These are people who, as Daniel Dennett suggests, are more likely to believe *in belief* than to believe in God.

The Christian church must respond to the challenge of the New Atheism with the full measure of conviction. We are reminded that the church has faced a constellation of theological challenges throughout its history. Then, as now, the task is to articulate, communicate, and defend the Christian faith with intellectual integrity and evangelistic urgency. We should not assume that this task will be easy, and we must also refuse to withdraw from public debate and private conversation in light of this challenge.

In the final analysis, the New Atheism presents the Christian church with a great moment of clarification. The New Atheists do, in the end, understand what they are rejecting. When Sam Harris defines true religion as any "belief in a supernatural agent or agents whose approval is to be sought," he understands what many mired in confusion do not. That is to say, even the New Atheists recognize that the only God that matters is a supernatural God—a personal God—who will judge. In the end, the existence of the supernatural, self-existent, and self-revealing God is the only adequate starting point for Christian theology. God possesses all of the perfections revealed in Scripture, or there is no coherent theology presented in the Bible.

The definition of "Christian" is also of crucial importance here. Harris defines a Christian as one who believes "that the Bible is the Word of God, that Jesus is the Son of God, and that only those who place their faith in Jesus will find salvation after death." Once again, he is much clearer here than many *Christians* are about what Christians are to believe. The New Atheists are certainly right about one very important thing—it's atheism or biblical theism. There is nothing in between.